FI JTERS

Other How To Books on jobs and careers

Finding a Job in Computers
How to Apply for a Job
How to Be a Freelance Journalist
How to Be a Freelance Sales Agent
How to Be a Freelance Secretary
How to Become an Au Pair
How to Do Voluntary Work Abroad
How to Find Temporary Work Abroad
How to Get a Job Abroad
How to Get a Job in Hotels & Catering
How to Get a Job in America
How to Get a Job in Australia
How to Get a Job in Europe
How to Get a Job in France
How to Get a Job in Germany
How to Get a Job in Travel & Tourism
How to Know Your Rights at Work
How to Manage Your Career
How to Market Yourself
How to Return to Work
How to Start a New Career
How to Work from Home
How to Work in an Office
How to Work in Retail
How to Work with Dogs
How to Work with Horses
How to Write a CV That Works
Living & Working in China
Surviving Redundancy
Working as a Holiday Rep
Working in Japan
Working on Contract Worldwide
Working on Cruise Ships

Other titles in preparation

The How To Series now contains more than 150 titles in the following categories:

Business Matters
Family Reference
Jobs & Careers
Living & Working Abroad
Student Handbooks
Successful Writing

Please send for a free copy of the latest catalogue for full details
(see back cover for address)

How To Books

JOBS & CAREERS

FINDING A JOB IN COMPUTERS

How to share in the information technology revolution

Stephen Harding

How To Books

By the same author

How to Write & Sell Computer Software

Dedication

This book is dedicated to my mother and father and to my two brothers—a true family.

Cartoons by Mike Flanagan

British Library Cataloguing-in-Publication data
A catalogue record for this book is available from the British Library.

First published in 1996 by How To Books Ltd, Plymbridge House, Estover Road, Plymouth PL6 7PZ, United Kingdom.
Tel: (01752) 202301. Fax: (01752) 202331.

Note: The material contained in this book is set out in good faith for general guidance and no liability can be accepted for loss or expense incurred as a result of relying in particular circumstances on statements made in the book. The laws and regulations are complex and liable to change, and readers should check the current position with the relevant authorities before making personal arrangements.

Produced for How To Books by Deer Park Productions.
Typeset by Kestrel Data, Exeter.
Printed and bound in Great Britain by Cromwell Press, Broughton Gifford, Melksham, Wiltshire.

Contents

List of Illustrations

Preface

Do you want a job in the computer industry? As a computer programmer perhaps, a systems analyst, or as a computer hardware engineer? Good. You have come to the right place.

Computers are everywhere nowadays. Around one in ten households in the UK now owns at least one and over half of all UK businesses are computerised.

Companies, individuals and organisations of all kinds are busily buying, installing and using new computer equipment and software at unprecedented rates. UK customers alone buy over two million personal computers every year and spend a phenomenal seven billion pounds every year on software and software related services. The market is huge—and growing fast.

Despite this, the companies and businesses that supply this market have a problem. **They cannot recruit enough suitable staff**.

In the UK and Europe, as well as in countries like the USA, Australia, New Zealand and Japan, the 'computer skills shortage' means that companies find it increasingly difficult to find and recruit skilled computer personnel in a job market where the number of vacancies on offer exceeds the number of people available to fill them.

The computer personnel most in demand are:

- computer programmers
- software engineers
- systems analysts
- computer engineers
- computer repair and maintenance staff
- computer support staff
- hardware and software training staff
- computer sales staff.

As a result, the rewards and salaries heaped on the individuals able to find and take up such positions have never been greater.

More importantly, the opportunities for enthusiastic, talented newcomers hoping to secure their first computing job are more abundant now than they have ever been.

Yet the computer press is bombarded with letters from disappointed people who, despite having made genuine efforts to secure their first computing job, have found it impossible. Their common claim is that employers only want to recruit experienced staff but that getting such experience is impossible if they cannot find employment. This well known but mythical 'catch 22' situation appears to them to be impassable. It is not.

Firstly, computing companies in the UK alone recruit over 20,000 individuals a year with little or no previous commercial computing experience. You just have to know how to become one of them. Secondly, there are innumerable ways to gain valuable, relevant and demonstrable computing experience outside of a full time computing job. You just have to know how.

So before reaching for your local newspaper or writing a host of speculative letters to local computing companies, take a little time to arm yourself with the valuable knowledge this book has to offer.

Initially dispelling the notion that a university degree and a wealth of previous computing experience are prerequisites to finding work in the computer industry, each chapter is geared towards preparing you for a real computing job—whatever your background, education or experience.

Successive chapters show the kinds of jobs that are available within the computer industry—especially to newcomers. They show how and where successful job candidates find real computing job vacancies, how they develop and then make the most of their computer skills and how they successfully apply for and take up computer related jobs.

Individual chapters show how the real professionals tailor their CVs specifically to finding work in the computer industry, how and where they are able to get free help and computer training, how they prepare for computer aptitude tests, how they prepare for and perform at interviews and how they assess and respond to job offers.

The final chapter deals with finding computer jobs abroad. There is an extensive country by country guide dedicated to providing information such as what particular computer skills are in demand in each country, average salary levels, the working and living conditions compared with those in the UK, and a wealth of extra factual information including numerous useful contact addresses both here and abroad, and valuable sources of further reading.

It is hoped that by reading this book you will become one of the 20,000 successful new computing job applicants every year—at the very least it will certainly help. However, at the end of the day it is down to you. It is your effort, enthusiasm, dedication and knowledge that will eventually win you the computing job you really want. Let's get to it.

Stephen Harding

IS THIS YOU?

Student	Fifth former	Sixth former
Undergraduate	Computer programmer	Intelligent
Thorough	Analytical	Meticulous
Computer enthusiast	PC owner	Computer gamer
Ambitious	Decisive	Hard working
Diligent	Industrious	Persevering
In tune with technology	Go-getter	Bored with your current job
Precise	Good listener	Effective communicator
Calm in a crisis	Courteous	Self starter
Ready for a challenge	Interested	Positive
Methodical	Perceptive	Self disciplined
Good negotiator	Confident	Trustworthy

1
Exploring the Computer Industry

Do you want a job in computers? Great. You are certainly reading the right book. There are many publications dealing with how to find jobs in general, but hardly any specifically geared to helping you find a job in the computer industry. This one is.

OVERVIEWING THE COMPUTER INDUSTRY

Although computers initially appeared during the 1940s and 1950s, job opportunities were, at that time, seldom available to anyone other than specialists. Up until the early 1980s this situation gradually improved as computers slowly began to proliferate and become more accessible and easy to use.

However, it was during the early 1980s, and particularly as the first usable business microcomputers came on to the market, that sales and the number of new jobs in the computer industry really began to increase rapidly. As job opportunities began to decline in traditional high employment industry areas such as manufacturing, engineering and administration, so newer, information technology related jobs have dramatically increased to take their place.

From humble beginnings just 40 or 50 years ago, computers can now be found in most areas of modern life. In particular computers are commonly found:

- in the home—with games and leisure software, word processing and educational software being the most popular

- in schools, colleges, universities and other educational establishments

- in offices, banks, insurance companies, government

establishments, gas, water and electricity companies, and businesses of all sizes

- in factories, power stations, research establishments, defence sites, manufacturing plants.

Indeed it is difficult to think of many areas of business or home life yet to be affected by the advance of the computer.

Relying on computers

Having made the transition from manual methods of working to using computer systems and having become committed to supplying products and services previously impossible without computers, many governments, factories, businesses and individuals have come to rely solely on the performance of their computer systems (and the staff that look after them) to remain in business.

Today the UK computer industry alone employs more than 400,000 people. By the year 2000 this figure is forecast to be 500,000—and to continue to grow. Job opportunities now, especially for newcomers, have never been greater.

However, our aim is to find **you** a job in computers, so let us take a look at some of the myths surrounding the computer industry and some of the many prospects it offers to enthusiastic and talented newcomers.

DISPELLING SOME MYTHS

Myth	*Right/wrong*
You need to have a degree in computing or maths to get a job in computers.	Wrong
You need at least three 'A' levels in applicable subjects to get a job in computers.	Wrong
At least one 'A' level?	Wrong
Surely at least good GCSEs are mandatory?	Wrong
Well, proven computer experience must be a prerequisite then?	Wrong

So anyone can get a job in computers? Wrong

So what does it take to secure a job in computers?

For individuals looking for their first job in the computer or information technology (IT) industry, many employers say that superior academic qualifications and previous commercial computing experience come second to having a strong, enthusiastic and demonstrable **interest in computers**. Solid academic qualifications certainly help and proven computing experience will definitely support job applications, but are no guarantees on their own of securing a suitable computer appointment.

Later in the book we will examine some practical steps that you can take to persuade employers that your interest and enthusiasm for computers and/or software override any lack of academic qualifications and lack of previous commercial computing experience.

Looking at IT opportunities and academic qualifications

Figure 1 gives a list of some of the many kinds of computing jobs widely taken up by those just beginning an IT career. Each type of job is shown with what employers generally consider to be the minimum level of academic achievement necessary to take up such positions. If candidates are unable to offer the minimum academic qualifications, then also shown is the number of years or months of previous computing experience that employers normally accept as an alternative. The various job titles themselves will be fully discussed in chapter 2.

Qualifications versus experience

Actually, most employers view things the other way around. They say that if candidates are unable to offer the minimum amount of previous computing experience, then as an alternative, they will consider candidates with the specified minimum level of academic qualifications.

To reinforce this point, as candidates' computing experience grows in their first job, their academic qualifications quickly become of much lesser importance to their employers. So, for example, if a candidate takes up a trainee programmer's position at the age of 16 with GCSE level qualifications, then after approximately twelve months' worth of on-the-job experience and training, the candidate could quickly progress to a full blown

Job title	GCSE	'A' levels	Degree	**OR** years' relevant experience (however gained)
Software related				
Trainee computer programmers	x	x	x	6 mths
Computer programmers		x	x	1
Software engineers		x	x	1.5–2
Software testers	x	x	x	any
Systems analysts			x	2
Hardware related				
Assembly and testing staff	x	x	x	1
Hardware engineers			x	3
Hardware maintenance and repair	x	x	x	1
Operators	x	x	x	1
Other				
Computer training		x	x	1
Customer support	x	x	x	1
Sales staff	x	x	x	any
Technical authors		x	x	3+
VDU operators	x	x	x	any
Total number of job titles accessible at each level	8	12	14	

Note 1. GCSE qualifications implies passes in around four subjects.

Note 2. 'A' Level qualifications implies passes at grade 'C' or above in two subjects.

Note 3. Degree level qualifications implies a pass at 2.2 or above.

Note 4. For some positions including computer sales, VDU operators and some customer support roles, educational requirements are desirable only and may be waived by employers altogether.

Fig. 1. Job titles and related qualifications.

computer programming position—without having to obtain any further academic qualifications.

Drawing conclusions

From Figure 1 it can be surmised that, although higher academic qualifications help in making a wider range of different computing jobs available to the individual, even those with basic GCSE qualifications have a wide range of IT jobs to aim at. Even if you have few or no formal academic qualifications, you can see that relevant computing experience in some form or other, and however gained, will more than compensate for any shortfall in academic achievement.

Did you know . . . ?

1. IT companies say that the biggest problem they face today is not finding or winning new business—it is being able to find and recruit suitable IT staff.
2. Around 20,000 people start their first job in the computer industry every year. Over half do not have academic qualifications higher than 'A' level standard. Many are not qualified even to GCSE standard.

Question time

Academic qualifications seem to be largely of secondary importance to employers in the computer industry. Is this really the case?
Yes, at least most of the time, and certainly if you:

- are over 25 years old, OR
- have two or more years' previous computing experience AND
- want to find computer related work in this country.

How much of an advantage will having a degree in computing science be?
Surprisingly not that much. For hardware related computing jobs, a computer science degree might be useful, provided the actual degree course contained a strong physics, maths or engineering bias. For other types of computer related work, employers are largely split as to the relevance of a computing science degree. Whereas some employers only recruit new staff with computer science degrees, others actively avoid offering work to computer science graduates, preferring instead to take arts, humanities or

foreign language graduates and to train them from scratch in the 'house' method of developing hardware, software and business solutions.

What and how many job opportunities are there in the computer industry for someone with less than the minimum number of GCSE qualifications?
Plenty—in fact up to 10,000 real job vacancy opportunities every year across the range of different job titles highlighted in Figure 1 above.

EXAMINING TODAY'S COMPUTER JOBS MARKET

The dramatic increases in computer related job vacancies seen in the late 1980s did slow noticeably during the 'recession' years of the early 1990s. However, at the time of writing, in the early part of 1996, the computer job market is buoyant again—in fact more buoyant than it has even been.

As a result, nearly all of the categories of job title shown in Figure 1 have experienced a marked upturn in demand for staff.

Surveying the computer jobs market

The computer jobs market is subject to all kinds of surveys. As a result of such surveys and the general increase in demand for suitable computer staff, a number of market trends are beginning to appear. The results of different surveys occasionally contradict each other but most are in agreement on several central themes:

- demand for quality computer staff has never been stronger
- as a consequence, salaries for most computer related jobs have tended to increase at a rate above that of inflation every year
- benefits, perks, bonuses and other payments over and above annual salary figures are also on the increase
- the long held view that you have to be male to secure a job in computing has been proved totally incorrect—in some areas of computing the number of women employed is much greater than the number of men

- on average a first time entrant into a computer related job tends to leave it again, usually for a better paid position with another computing company, within the first two years—thus leaving a vacancy suitable for a 'first timer' again.

All of the above findings represent good news for newcomers looking for their first job in computing. However, job applicants beware. Other findings may not be so appealing. For example, of the 20,000 or so new computing jobs on offer every year, around half are taken up by candidates with a university degree. In addition, competition amongst job applicants at all levels is extremely fierce. To cap it all, companies surveyed have said that finding *suitable* staff is what is most difficult, not finding staff in general.

Defining a 'suitable' computer job applicant

Companies and businesses, rather than buying and operating a number of different makes of computer, tend to adopt only one or two. Similarly, most also use comparatively few software packages out of the many thousands available. In this context companies view 'suitable' applicants as those having specific and in depth experience of the particular hardware and software packages they use.

'Suitable' applicants are always **well presented, articulate, intelligent, flexible** and **enjoy working in a team environment**. In some cases, 'suitable' candidates are also under 45 and prepared to travel. Occasionally, 'suitable' also means 'university graduate'.

GETTING YOURSELF ORGANISED

There has never been a better time to look for a job in computers. Conversely, never before have there been as many people looking for their first computing job.

Competition is fierce and if you are to secure that computing job you really want then you will need to **plan to succeed**. Getting organised to look for IT work is your first task. Concentrate initially on getting interviews. Then concentrate on preparing for and handling them as competently and professionally as possible.

Getting organised means:

- having a positive approach to looking for work in computers
- determining the right kind of computing job for you
- determining your 'job search area'—the geographical boundaries within which you will look for work
- determining a profile of the kind of company you would like to work for and how many of these companies exist within your job search area
- regularly looking out for computing job adverts
- seeking and noting the advice given by careers counsellors, Job Centres, and making the most of the many types of free computing and IT training courses on offer
- establishing a daily routine geared towards finding work.

Having a positive approach

Although luck can occasionally be a factor when looking for work, on the whole computing jobs will not come to you. A **positive approach** to looking for computer work is essential. Rather than waiting for computing work to come your way, go out and actively look for work, be confident, refuse to accept that obstacles and barriers are insurmountable and above all, prepare to devote 100 per cent of your effort to identifying and then pursuing as many suitable and available job opportunities as possible.

Identifying the type of computing job for you

The computer industry is vast. All kinds of widely different jobs are available. From computer programmers to hardware technicians and from assembly staff through to computer salespeople and training instructors, with such a wide choice it is necessary to narrow down the range of jobs you might be prepared to apply for.

By making a list of the computing job titles you are most interested in and feel you are most suited for, and by restricting your search for work to just the job titles you have listed, you will:

Board level

Overall company strategy

Hardware	**Software**	**Services**
Design	Analysis	Customer support
Test	Design	Training
Manufacture	Specification	Consultancy
Maintain	Programming	Bespoke services
Repair	Testing	
Operations	Maintenance	
	Upgrading	

Sales	**Admin**
Hardware	Personnel
Software	Finance
Services	Premises
Marketing	Equipment
Advertising	Other
New business	

Fig. 2. A large computer company's main departments and their responsibilities.

- increase your overall chance of finding work
- ensure that you don't spend unnecessary effort on applying for jobs you have no real interest in or chance of getting
- be able to focus on finding the type of job you really want and for which you are most suited.

Identifying the **right computing job for you** is so important that most of chapter 2 is devoted to helping you find it. In the meantime, make an initial list of computing job titles you think you may be interested in and possibly suited to. Figure 3 shows some common types of computing jobs to help you choose. Do not be restricted by this list, however. By all means write down any type of computing job title you think might interest you, even if it is not on the list.

Determining your job search area

Where you live will, in many circumstances, determine where you look for work. You will first need to decide where you are prepared to work. This involves drawing up a **job search area** within which you are prepared to travel or move in order to take up a computing job.

Determine your job search area by writing down the different methods of travel available to you, how much they might cost and how much time you might be prepared to spend travelling to and from work. Bear in mind particularly:

- **cost** of travel—how much it will cost to get to and from work each day
- how much **time** will you have to spend getting to and from your place of work
- **weather**—this can affect your choice no matter how you intend to get to work
- **reliability**—can you be sure to reach work on time every day?

Listing potential employers

Who you will work for is every bit as important as where you will

Software related

Trainee computer programmer

Computer programmer

Software engineer

Software tester

Systems analyst

Software designer

Software user

Hardware related

Hardware assembly and test engineer

Hardware engineer

Hardware maintenance and repair engineer

Computer operator

Hardware installer

Network/communications expert

Computer user

Other

Computer trainer

Customer support

Computer/software sales

Technical author

VDU operator

Fig. 3. Computing job titles.

work. All sorts of companies and businesses use, develop, sell and program computers. Each can offer many different opportunities for computer job hunters. Do not restrict your search simply to software houses or computer manufacturers or to companies directly involved with computers as their primary business. Some of the largest and most accessible employers in your area may *use* computers rather than actually manufacturing them, selling them or writing software for them. Government departments, local councils and the Armed Services are all good examples of large IT employers with extensive computing departments who predominantly use computers rather than attempting to make a commercial profit from them.

Start by listing the potential IT employers in your job search area. You can do this by:

- consulting the *Yellow Pages* or other local telephone directories and listing the names and addresses of local businesses you know or think may use, program, maintain, sell or manufacture hardware, software or computer related services

- reading job advertisements and noting the names of companies advertising computer oriented vacancies

- asking for advice at local Job Centres or from careers guidance officers

- using the TV and radio to note details of companies advertising computing vacancies or to note details of companies who are shown to have an IT involvement of some kind

- visiting your local library. Several publications exist, usually in the reference section, which list computer companies, where they are, the range of hardware and software they use and the particular areas of business in which they operate. A good example of such a publication is *The Computer Users Year Book*.

Further reading

The Computer Users Year Book and *The Software Users Year Book* (VNU Business Publications, tel: (0171) 316 9637) and available at most reference libraries.

DRAWING UP A PLAN OF ACTION

Now that you have in hand a list of potential employers in your area, the next stage is to draw up a plan of action for finding, researching, training for and then applying for computer related work. Your plan of action should be especially geared towards:

- finding work broadly in line with one or more of the types of computing jobs you listed earlier as being interested in and potentially suited for
- finding computing work within your identified job search area
- initially contacting the IT companies you already have on your 'list of potential employers'.

In particular, you are interested in knowing which of these potential employers are currently looking for new computing staff and which ones, although perhaps not actively looking at present, would be interested in interviewing you anyway, with a view to satisfying their future requirements.

On a day to day basis, your plan of action means:

- reading newspapers, visiting Job Centres, careers offices and libraries in order to:

  – find new computing opportunities within your local job search area

  – add any additional company names and addresses of IT employers to your list of potential employers
- contacting companies and potential employers on your list with a speculative letter or by telephone
- speaking with friends, relatives and your existing 'contacts' already working in computer related jobs.

Useful things to have

- newspapers containing adverts for computer jobs
- specialist job hunting magazines and newspapers and computing-specific trade newspapers and journals
- pens, paper, envelopes, stamps
- access to a word processor or computer—access to a quality laser printer would also be a distinct advantage
- a telephone—access to a fax machine or to a computer equipped with a modem might also prove useful
- a notebook in which to record names, addresses and other details of potential employers in the computing field
- a diary
- a 'job file' for holding copies of all letters sent out and replies received
- a book or magazine containing 'logic', aptitude or intelligence tests. Tests like these are commonly used by computing companies to assess candidates' suitability for computer related work
- a radio or TV—often an overlooked source of advertisements for computer related work and information on the companies that use IT
- a local library membership card
- a list of local employers and businesses likely to manufacture, write software for, use, distribute, repair or sell computers.

CASE STUDIES

Introduction

In order to illustrate some of the right and wrong ways of seeking a job in computers, let us now introduce three fictional characters, all intending to find a job in computers for the first time. Each has a different blend of background and experience and will adopt their own personal approach to solving the problems they confront along the way. Successive chapters will chart their progress and the consequences of the actions and decisions they take.

Dave Ellis leaves school with an interest in computers

Dave is an ambitious but realistic fifth form student who decides that a job in computers is much more of a priority than further studies at school or university. Already owning a computer which he uses mainly to write his own small software programs and for playing the latest computer games, Dave knows that he will probably have to start at the bottom and work up from there. Confident, likeable and, despite his obvious lack of commercial experience, already quite adept at writing software, Dave hopes to find work as a trainee programmer with a small, but reputable, software company preferably within a ten-mile radius of his home.

Jenny Williams studies computer science and business studies

Jenny is a 21 year old, talented undergraduate coming towards the end of the final year of a combined computing and business studies degree course. Although she is interested in business and commercial problems, Jenny's real passion is for computers. Indeed, she has written and used software on her own personal computer for the previous three years and has always intended to pursue a computing career once she completes her university studies. Despite this, Jenny is also a realist. She knows that, even as a graduate, finding work in the fiercely competitive computer job market will not be at all easy and that, although she is prepared to work almost anywhere in the country, she will still need all the help she can get if she is going to succeed.

Steve Morton seeks to change his career

Steve has worked in the offices of a large insurance company ever since leaving school with 'A' levels. Widely thought of as an asset to his department, Steve has nevertheless grown tired of the same routine and feels that, after ten years, a career change is now necessary. Steve has always enjoyed, and been particularly good at, operating and getting the most from his employer's computer, and he especially enjoys training new staff—an activity he has been responsible for over the past two years. Steve does not personally own a computer, nor does he have any knowledge of how to write computer software, but he nevertheless feels that these need not be barriers to finding a more computer oriented job. Ideally, Steve wants to find work within 35 miles of his home.

DISCUSSION POINTS

1. Why do you want a job in computing?

2. What interests, skills and hobbies do you have or pursue which, in addition to your academic qualifications, might help to persuade an IT employer to recruit you in preference to other job applicants?

3. Are you really committed to finding work in computers? If so, where are you prepared to work geographically and how can you ensure that your search for work concentrates solely on employers in this area?

2
Identifying the Right Job for You

We have already seen and listed some of the job titles which we think we may be interested in or suited for. So let us now find out a little more about the job titles we have listed.

CONSIDERING YOUR SKILLS AND INTERESTS

Your best chances of finding computer related work will be in areas where you already have some experience or knowledge.

If you have a computer at school, college or at home, which above all else you enjoy writing software programs for, then this strongly suggests that you would be far more suitable for a job as a **computer programmer** or trainee programmer than you would for a job as, say, a hardware engineer. Similarly, if your interest is in exploring, fault finding, building or repairing circuit boards and other electronic or electrical equipment, then you would probably be best suited to some kind of job related to **building or repairing computers** or their components.

Let us now look in more detail at some of the different jobs a career in computing can offer. Before we do, though, it is important to be aware that different companies use different job titles to refer to basically the same kind of computing position. As far as possible, the most common or generic job titles have been used along with their less common alternatives listed in italics below.

SPECIALISING IN COMPUTER HARDWARE

Specialising in hardware means specialising in the design, development, assembly, maintenance and repair of the computer equipment itself, rather than the software that runs on it. In this context, computer equipment means the computer itself (and all of its components) and any or all of the following:

- printers, scanners, monitors
- telecommunications equipment
- computer cabling
- computer networks
- any other equipment commonly used in conjunction with a computer.

Hardware engineers

Hardware designers, hardware developers, hardware technicians

Hardware engineers rarely write software. Their primary task is to develop machines and devices that are as a whole capable of running software or which provide an easy means for humans to use or operate them. A hardware engineer can typically be involved in a range of hardware related tasks such as:

- hardware research and development work
- designing new or modifying existing designs of individual components
- fault finding and diagnosing failures in new pieces of equipment
- building scale and full size models of computers and their components.

New hardware engineers normally need at least a university degree, preferably in electronic engineering, physics, maths or another closely related subject. In return, starting salaries are between £15,000 and £25,000 per annum depending on the employer and geographic location.

Hardware assembly and test engineers

Test engineers, assembly staff

Hardware assembly and test engineers typically build complete systems or parts of systems from components which have been designed and developed by hardware engineers. For a computer, a typical assembly engineer's job involves building the complete computer system, assembling such components as circuit boards, disk drives, power supply units, fans and other smaller components to make the completed unit.

Assembly and test engineers are recruited at many levels. With good GCSEs, many larger companies and some government departments are prepared to take on a limited number of apprentices and train them in this kind of work. Typical starting salaries are in the range of £9,000–£15,000.

Hardware maintenance and repair engineers

Hardware maintenance and repair engineers provide computing companies and IT departments with services such as:

- 'on site' repair or replacement for their computer equipment
- fault finding and fault diagnosis, followed by repair
- computer equipment servicing and maintenance
- hardware installation, wiring, cabling and removal.

This type of position is very varied, involving both office or workshop based work and a fair amount of travel to customer sites. Maintenance and repair staff on the whole are recruited at the same level and paid at around the same rates as assembly and test engineers.

Computer operators

Operations staff, operators

Computer operators are responsible for the manual tasks associated with the day to day running of larger computer installations. These tasks typically include physically loading disks and tapes into computers and paper into printers, changing printer ribbons, and removing and distributing printed reports. Computer operators are also responsible for invoking and running programs, often at specific times of the day (or night) and for ensuring that these programs are run in a prearranged and specific order.

Operators are recruited at all levels; relevant previous experience or a strong interest in the practical aspects of running computer systems is normally viewed by employers as being of far more value than academic achievements. Salaries are in the range £10,000–£20,000 depending on the level of the position.

WRITING COMPUTER SOFTWARE

By far the largest number of available computing positions in the UK tend to be for staff required for **software related** work—over 16,000 every year.

Software packages, sometimes known as 'applications' or 'programs', enable their owners to harness and direct the huge processing power and capabilities of modern computers to solve real life business problems or for leisure purposes.

Computer applications include software which:

- controls devices and machinery such as industrial robots, manufacturing equipment, and washing machines
- facilitates the storage and easy retrieval of computer data (or information)
- enables businesses to perform word processing, efficiently reconcile financial accounts and pay employees' salaries
- permits artists, designers and engineers to create images, computer models, and scaled drawings of their products or designs
- provides entertainment and leisure—computer games for example
- is custom written, bespoke or 'tailor made' for use specifically within a single company—like a membership registration system for automobile associations, a school time-tabling system or specialist insurance-quoting software unique to an individual insurance company.

Trainee computer programmers

Trainee computer programmers learn how to write software to run on computers. Most often trainee programmers work on a piece of software under the direct supervision of a more experienced computer programmer. During their period of training, many individuals often have the opportunity to write completely new software from scratch and to continue to work on it until the software is finished.

Smaller businesses tend to recruit trainee programmers with four or five GCSEs, whereas some of the larger companies and government departments prefer to recruit trainees with 'A' level qualifications. Occasionally graduates are also recruited. Starting salaries for trainee programmers fall in the range £7,000–£14,000, though trainees can often expect to achieve promotion to fully fledged computer programmer within 6–24 months.

Computer programmers

Applications programmers, software developers, programmers, software authors

Computer programmers develop new software programs, often from scratch, and maintain, modify and improve existing software.

Computer programmers require good analytical and logic skills. They need to be good problem solvers and, as well as having a technical programming ability, they also need to be able to communicate their ideas and solutions to others.

Normally working in teams of between two and 30, first time computer programmers are most often recruited with 'A' level qualifications or higher.

Contrary to popuar belief, maths and computing science qualifications do not greatly benefit computer programmers and graduates are not necessarily at much more of an advantage than anyone else when applying for programming positions.

Typical starting salaries for first time computer programmers fall in the range £9,000–£16,000 depending on the location and nature of the work.

Software engineers

Similar to computer programmers in many respects, software engineers normally work on software which:

- controls machinery or automated equipment—washing machines, weapon systems, space rockets, industrial robots

- is highly scientific, mathematical or biased towards engineering or work of a highly technical nature—CAD (computer aided design) systems, computer models of real life, simulations, weather monitoring systems, fault diagnosis, space and defence systems.

Software engineering is much more of a controlled process than computer programming. Whereas the consequences of failure in a normal application may simply result in inconvenience or a telephone call to a local supplier, failures in 'engineered software' could result in loss of life, property or some other catastrophic loss.

Consequently, the individuals employed as first time software engineers tend to have at least 'A' level qualifications and, more often than not, university degrees. Starting salaries range between £12,000 and £19,000.

Systems analysts

Software analysts, software designers, analyst/programmers

Systems analysts provide the input for the work carried out by computer programmers and software engineers. Typically, their jobs involve analysing current business practices and systems or customer requirements, and then looking for and presenting more efficient ways of achieving company or customer aims using a computer.

Systems analysts need:

- logical minds
- a knowledge of business as well as of computers and software
- imagination and the ability to develop ideas
- an ability to communicate with people of all levels effectively.

Many companies only recruit systems analysts with degree level qualifications. However, good 'A' level standard qualifications coupled with previous business knowledge can often be just as acceptable. In recent years the roles of systems analysts and computer programmers have gradually merged. The result in some companies is that a new role, that of 'analyst/programmer', has evolved. Average starting salaries fall between £12,000 and £20,000.

Software testers

Software testers are responsible for ensuring that software packages work exactly as intended and specified, that they are easy to use and that they perform adequately (run at acceptable speeds) on the computers they are intended to run on.

Software testers also 'quality assure' software ensuring that it works in a common and consistent way. This is especially important when it is realised that as many as 30–50 computer programmers or software engineers could have written different parts of the same software package.

Despite the recent focus on software quality within many organisations, the task of testing software alone is often not enough to warrant employing full time staff. Therefore, where software testers are employed they tend also to be involved in other tasks as well—such as writing software manuals or training users.

Software testers are recruited with all levels of academic achievement and first time testers can expect starting salaries of between £8,000 and £15,000 per year.

SUPPORTING AND TRAINING COMPUTER USERS

Despite recent advances, both computers and the software that runs on them are still comparatively complex and difficult to use. As a consequence, there is a strong and growing requirement for individuals to fill customer/user training and support roles.

Trainers

Training instructors, tutors, computer training specialists

Trainers typically instruct users on how to use their computers and their existing software to solve common business problems effectively. Training can range from simple instruction, such as how to turn a computer on, to highly specialised training such as teaching software engineers how to write software that controls the computer's sound system or disk drive.

In computer training, the ability to communicate thoughts, ideas and methods is every bit as important as a sound technical knowledge.

Depending on the level of training undertaken, most companies are prepared to take 'A' level and degree standard candidates, so long as they can already demonstrate:

- proven knowledge and experience in a specific computing area
- excellent communications skills
- lots of patience.

Starting salaries vary widely—between £10,000–£20,000 depending on the position.

Customer support

Software support, hardware support, technical support, help desk staff, pre-sales support staff, post-sales support staff

Customer support staff provide help and advice to existing users, customers or potential buyers.

Though prior technical experience is desirable for some computer support positions, most support staff tend to receive on-the-job training in the particular hardware or software being sold, installed or used at the time. As a result, academic qualifications tend not to be as important as the ability to learn, the ability to think clearly and logically to solve technical problems under pressure and, most importantly, the ability to talk to, reassure and listen to customers.

Expect to find support staff with all levels of academic qualifications and at salaries ranging from £7,000 to £16,000.

SELLING COMPUTERS, SOFTWARE AND SERVICES

Sales staff

Computer salespeople, sales engineers, sales representatives

Sales staff are arguably the most important individuals in a computing or software company. Without them, no other types of position could exist. Sales staff, hired by hardware manufacturers, IT software companies, computer services companies and retailers, are responsible for:

- attracting customers
- selling to customers
- keeping customers.

Sales staff should ideally have an outgoing, confident personality, an in-depth knowledge of their product, and a strong appreciation of the customer's needs. On-the-job training is most often given and a candidate's performance at interview, coupled with his/her demonstrable communication and selling skills, will largely outweigh any lack of academic achievement. Salaries vary widely and many employers operate commission based salary schemes.

LOOKING AT OTHER TYPES OF COMPUTER JOBS

Technical authors

Technical writers, documentation staff

Technical authors typically write the hardware, software and training manuals which accompany a company's main product or products. They also provide written instructions, and in some cases oral tuition, to users and customers, in order to ease the introduction or continued use of a hardware or software product.

Although on-the-job training is given to many technical authors, the primary requirements are good, clear writing skills and an ability to overview complex systems before logically breaking them down and presenting their constituent parts in an easy-to-understand and logically ordered written form.

Technical authors often combine the technical writing element of their jobs with other tasks such as hardware or software testing, quality assurance and user training.

Starting salaries fall in the range £8,000–£15,000.

VDU operators

VDU operators, though perhaps not strictly employees in the computing industry itself, nevertheless tend to use computers for much of their working day, and are therefore included here for completeness.

VDU operators typically enter information into a computer via a keyboard or some other input device. Around half of the nation's businesses use computers in some way or other and the number of staff employed by these businesses to operate them on a day to day basis is growing steadily.

There are openings for all levels of staff in this line of work. No formal academic qualifications are required to use the VDUs themselves. Both qualifications and salaries will largely be determined by the exact nature of the job itself.

Did you know . . . ?

1. There are more vacancies for computer programmers and software engineers than there are for any other type of computer related work, with the possible exception of VDU operators.
2. Some computer companies and software houses regard having a university degree as a disadvantage when applying for some kinds of computer related jobs.
3. Special aptitude tests often precede interviews for computing related jobs. Widely feared and often failed by even established and experienced computer professionals, aptitude tests are nevertheless designed to help employers discover which of their job applicants have logical, structured and organised thought processes.

Question time

What GCSE, 'A' level and degree level subjects are most appropriate for a career in computers?

At GCSE level: Maths, computer science, English, physics, any foreign language.

At 'A' level: Maths, statistics, physics, English, computer science, information technology, business studies, any foreign language.

At degree level:

For hardware related jobs: Maths, physics, engineering, some computer science degrees.

For non hardware related computer jobs: any degree is acceptable. Many employers actually prefer graduates with non computing related degrees.

What value do vocational qualifications have in the computer industry?

Vocational qualifications are those which are obtained by learning and demonstrating skills directly relevant to the area of employment associated with the subject. For computing, studying for a vocational qualification such as a National Vocational Qualification (NVQ), a Business and Technology Education Council (BTEC) qualification or a City and Guilds certificate would mean having, for example, to write a small software package, perhaps by using a personal computer, or assembling, repairing and maintaining real computer equipment. Vocational qualifications are becoming more acceptable to employers in the computer industry. Many IT employers, keen to ensure that candidates have more practical rather than academic knowledge of their subject, are often happier to consider candidates with vocational qualifications such as NVQs or BTECs over those with purely academic qualifications like 'A' levels.

CASE STUDIES

Dave wants to be a trainee computer programmer

Always realistic and level headed, Dave thinks that the main barriers to securing full time work as a trainee computer programmer are his three GCSE level qualifications, the apparent scarcity of opportunities for trainees, and the alarmingly high number of applicants for computer related job vacancies that arise locally. Nevertheless, Dave has decided that sixth form study could only be contemplated if a total lack of suitable computer opportunities forces him to do so.

To counter each of his three perceived obstacles, Dave plans to make the most of any free help or computer training available, to emphasise that his highest graded GCSE is in computer studies, to research the computing job market to find the maximum number of trainee programmer vacancies, and to find some way of distinguishing his job application and personal details from those of all the other job applicants.

Jenny worries about computer aptitude tests

Jenny is initially undecided about whether to try for a programming or a systems analysis position. In fact, she quite likes the idea of trying for both. Studying a combined business studies and computing degree, Jenny feels that either type of position will suit her skills. Armed with the knowledge that over a half of all new computing jobs go to graduates, Jenny is nevertheless prepared to counter the three main difficulties that she sees standing between her and a full time computing job. Namely, her lack of real business or commercial experience, the problem of finding suitable computing vacancies advertised in all parts of the UK and the problem of convincing potential employers that she, above all others, is the right candidate for the job. She is also concerned and worried by the possibility that she may be required to take a computer aptitude test. Although already a fairly competent computer programmer and likely to gain a good degree in a relevant subject, Jenny has never been confident about taking these kind of logic or intelligence tests and realises that failure in these could rule her out of many jobs before even being interviewed.

Steve feels confident of finding a job in computers

Although Steve has never worked in a full time computing job of any kind since leaving school with 'A' levels ten years previously, he nevertheless feels quietly confident about his chances of finding a more computer oriented job. This confidence stems from the fact that, although his 'A' level grades are lower than average, he can offer potential employers real evidence of actual business and commercial experience over a ten year period. He also feels he can demonstrate stability of previous employment and concrete evidence of the fact that his current job involves using computers on a daily basis as well as training and helping new staff in their use. In addition, and as a computer user, Steve also feels he can offer potential employers a 'customer's' view of the software business.

With no specific computer programming experience or specialist technical knowledge, Steve thinks that a user support position or even a sales role of some kind will be the best type of computing position to aim for. He also has to bear in mind the question of salary and job location. With a young family and a mortgage, Steve is particularly concerned to find work which offers a competitive salary and which falls within a reasonable travelling distance of his home.

DISCUSSION POINTS

1. Given the wide variety of computing jobs available, which ones do you feel you are particularly well suited for and interested in?

2. What do you feel are your main barriers to finding a job in computers and how do you intend to combat these?

3. Apart from salary, what else are you looking to gain from the types of IT jobs you are interested in?

3
Getting Free Help and Computer Training

Employers within the computer industry are crying out for suitably qualified computer staff. The shortage of suitable skilled people is cited by them as one of the biggest problems the computer industry faces.

Explaining the 'skills shortage'

Within the computer industry this problem, widely known as the 'skills shortage', results from IT employers having more vacancies on offer than they can fill with suitably qualified staff.

Skills shortages, particularly acute in the mid to late 1980s, became less of a problem during the recession years of the early 1990s. However, at the time of writing (early 1996), skills shortages are back again with a vengeance. Industry forecasters predict that the current overall skills shortage will continue to plague employers until at least the year 2002 and probably for a while after this.

What is bad news for IT employers is truly great news for computer job hunters. Skills shortages in the computer industry mean that:

- fewer suitable candidates apply for a larger number of computing job vacancies
- the overall level of skills and experience of candidates applying for computer related jobs is relatively lower than normal
- IT employers in general experience an increase in staff turnover (the rate at which staff join and then leave)
- the effect of more frequent internal promotions ripples down through company staff hierarchies and inevitably results in

more junior and middle level positions becoming vacant. These are the positions which tend to be filled by first time computer job seekers

- salary and remuneration levels tend to rise more quickly than normal.

Back to the real world . . .

Despite the skills shortage and its effects, as a computer job seeker you will nevertheless still face, and have to deal with, two age old but still critically important problems:

1. How to find suitable job vacancies.
2. How to ensure you are skilled enough and therefore suitable enough to have a reasonable chance of securing a job vacancy.

These two problems, faced by millions of job seekers before you, now confront you. Fortunately, help is at hand.

MAKING THE MOST OF THE CAREERS SERVICE

If you are currently at school, college or university, then it is likely that your establishment has a **careers office or officer** of some kind. Frequently, larger employers too have trained personnel staff ready to advise employees on the best way to manage their careers.

It is the job of a careers officer to advise people about suitable careers and, once this is established, to help them prepare for work in their chosen area.

Though careers officers do not tend to specialise in any one area of industry, more and more are becoming acutely aware of the growth of opportunities in the computer and IT sectors. They are able to provide:

- advice on the range of computing jobs available

- advice on how and where to study for the qualifications required for such jobs and how to acquire and practise computing skills outside of a full time computing job

- information on where to look for local and national IT related job vacancies

- verbal advice on how to find and approach IT employers
- lists of local and not so local IT employers
- advice on how to handle computer aptitude tests and formal interview situations.

Their help is free if you ask for it and if you do genuine efforts will be made on your behalf. Many careers officers also maintain strong links with local employers and may even be able to secure you an interview as a result. So, at the very least, consider making the most of your careers service if you have one.

USING JOB CENTRES

Job Centres, situated in most major towns and cities in the UK, provide a wealth of free help and advice across the whole employment spectrum.

For people explicitly looking for work in the computer industry, Job Centres offer:

- A wide range of current IT job vacancies and information. Situated in the 'Professional and Technical' section, these vacancies are likely to be for mainly local computing jobs. However, national and overseas computing job vacancies are also displayed from time to time.
- A free Executive Recruitment Service, designed explicitly to match professional people with suitable professional (including IT) job vacancies.
- A free Employment Service Programme consisting of detailed and practical advice on how to impress employers with written job applications, CVs, and at interviews.
- A 'Job Club' service which gives qualifying individuals free access to newspapers, stamps, paper, envelopes, photocopiers, computerised word processors and quality laser printing facilities.

- A vocational training programme run by Training and Enterprise Councils (TECs), providing individuals with access to IT and other training opportunities through an established network of organisations and employers. Typical vocational qualifications supported include NVQs and BTECs in Computing or Information Technology.

- Training Access Points (TAPs). These 'arcade game' style machines, situated both in Job Centres and many local libraries, are designed to provide local people with access to a database of local training and educational opportunities. They cost nothing to use and specific sections cater for training in computing and IT.

- An information centre—free leaflets, periodicals and books covering amongst others, jobs, careers, qualifications and training in IT related work.

Using the Employment Service to find computing work overseas

Most Job Centres have an **overseas section** which is devoted to supplying the latest overseas job vacancies to those searching for work abroad.

However, if your main aim is to find computing work overseas, the Employment Service also runs a more specialised department, known as the Overseas Placement Unit (OPU) which is responsible for coordinating activities with regard to helping UK citizens to find work both inside and outside of the European Union (EU).

Workers from the EU are free to live and work without work permits in any of the following EU countries:

Belgium	Italy
Denmark	Luxembourg
France	Portugal
Germany	Spain
Greece	The Netherlands
Ireland	United Kingdom

For computing job vacancies outside the EU an Overseas Labour Section (OLS) based in London may also be able to give advice on such things as work permits, immigration and emigration.

Useful addresses

The Employment Service, Overseas Placement Unit, 4th Floor, Steel City House, c/o Moorfoot, Sheffield S1 4PQ. Tel: (01742) 596051/2.

The Department of Employment, Overseas Labour Section, Caxton House, Tothill Street, London SW1H 9NA. Tel: (0171) 273 5336.

The Home Office, Immigration and Nationality Department, Lunar House, Wellesley Road, Croydon CR9 2BY. Tel: (0181) 686 0688.

TRAINING TO SUCCEED

Academic qualifications such as GCSE, 'A' levels and university degrees will always support your application for computer related work. Vocational qualifications such as NVQs, GNVQs, City and Guilds and BTEC are widely recognised by employers in the computer industry as highly applicable and relevant. However, to really impress computer employers and therefore give yourself the highest chance of securing computer related work, you must be able to demonstrate a **working knowledge** of the computer hardware and software packages that they actually use on a day to day basis.

So, for example, for software related positions calling for applicants with a knowledge of VISUAL BASIC and Windows 95, there is every likelihood that individuals with a practical working knowledge of these two software products, even if they have few academic qualifications, will be strongly preferred over graduates with no previous knowledge of these key skills.

Key computer skills win key computer jobs

The above example is typical of the way the computer industry recruits new staff. The view is that no matter how highly qualified individuals are from an academic viewpoint, they are of little use to companies if they do not have the specific computer or software skills required.

Even with hardware related jobs where, on the whole, academic qualifications are more highly valued by employers, preference will normally be given to those who can demonstrate a good blend of both academic and key technical skills.

Adopting an alternative approach to finding computer work

In view of this, rather than dwell on the importance of such things as university degrees, applicable 'A' levels and GCSE qualifications, the computer job seeker is well advised to adopt a different approach to finding computer work.

Tasks

1. Find out which hardware and software skills are most in demand by employers within your job search area.
2. List the skills you have found according to their popularity (the number of job vacancies specifying these skills as being required). Also list the IT employers you have found. Add any new ones to your list of potential employers.
3. For each of the skills in greatest demand, determine the ease and the cost involved in learning them—we will find out how to learn them and how much it costs later. Also try to determine how suitable you might be to learning and using these skills.
4. Depending on your preferences, select a skill or set of skills you feel will make you as an individual most in demand by the widest range of computer employers in your job search area, and which would be relatively inexpensive and most practical to learn.
5. If feasible, do everything you can to learn the skill(s) you have selected in the shortest period of time.
6. When you are confident enough in your ability to practise your new computer skills, concentrate on applying for jobs with the companies on your list that you already know use or require them.

For individuals with established and key computer skills, only task six on the above list is relevant. If no local computing companies can be found who use the skills you already possess, consider extending your job search area before, as a last resort, returning to task one on the above list.

Let us now look at each of the above tasks in detail and consider some of the practical steps that can be taken to achieve them.

Finding out which hardware and software skills are most in demand

It makes good sense to find out what **key computing skills** are most in demand locally, nationally and particularly within your own job search area. This will ensure that you concentrate on acquiring only the skills for positions you would be able to take up should they be offered. So just how can you find out which computing skills are most in demand?

You can do this by:

- studying computer job advertisements in local and national newspapers and noting down the number and frequency with which certain computing skills, models of computer and software packages are mentioned
- talking to friends and colleagues already in the computer industry or who own computers at home
- talking to computer and software retailers, to local employers and to local computer recruitment agencies
- studying and analysing popular computer magazines
- reading the computer trade press who regularly survey and publish listings of the skills currently in greatest demand by other computer employers
- visiting local staff recruitment agencies and Job Centres and browsing through their computer related vacancy lists.

Listing and ordering 'in demand' computing skills

The next step is to list and order your findings so that the popular computer skills, computer models and software packages are at the top of your list.

Figure 4 is a comprehensive, though by no means definitive, list of some of the specific computing skills most in demand by UK employers at the beginning of 1996.

Determining the best and easiest skills to learn

This is possibly the most difficult of our six tasks to achieve because it requires individual judgment. Also, the skills easiest and most convenient to learn for one will be completely unsuitable and inconvenient for another. In general, however, the cheapest, easiest and most convenient skills to learn will be those which can be learned by using a **personal computer** (PC) in some way. The proliferation of PCs in the UK and worldwide means that they:

Hardware

Personal computers and components

PC networks and communications

Client server technology

PC based software skills

C/C++, Windows 3.X/Windows 95/MS–DOS, Visual BASIC, any Microsoft Office application including ACCESS, WORD, and EXCEL; Lotus 123, Lotus Word Pro, WordPerfect Quattro Pro, Paradox, any communications, networking or groupware software, Lotus Notes, SQL database language

Mini computer based software skills

UNIX, VMS, INGRES, SQL, RPG, ORACLE, 'C', Windows NT, 'C++'

Mainframe based software skills

COBOL, DB2, CICS

Design methodologies

SSADM Version 4, Prince, Yourdon

Fig. 4. Computing skills most in demand now.

- are now relatively cheap to buy
- are easy to access, use and learn with
- run software commonly used in the office as well as at home
- are far more popular and widespread with computer related employers than probably any other type of computer system.

Fortunately for us, the cost of PCs and PC based software also dictates to a large extent the cost and therefore the ease of learning of both hardware and many of the more 'in demand' software related computer skills.

Figure 5 lists the skills that are likely to be relatively cheap, easy to obtain, and in greatest demand by UK based computer employers.

Bear in mind that the ease and cost of acquiring new computer skills is also largely proportional to the numbers of future job applicants likely to be in the process of acquiring these skills. In time, as the number of skilled individuals rises, so will the difficulty and competition involved with finding and securing work using these skills.

The trick, if possible, is to identify, acquire, develop and use your new skills in the shortest possible time frame—before the competition does.

Acquiring the right computer skills

Your next task is to set about acquiring and practising the skills you have selected as being the ones most likely to secure you your first computing job in the shortest possible time and at the minimum cost.

You should assume that you need to have acquired and practised your new computer skills to a level sufficient to secure employment in the computer industry, **within six to twelve months**. Any longer than this and the rapidly changing computer skills market is likely to have moved on to such an extent that the skills you originally identified as being in demand are likely not to be in demand any more.

Hardware

Personal computers and components

PC networks and communications

PC based software skills

C/C+ +, Windows 3.X/Windows 95/MS–DOS, Visual BASIC, any Microsoft Office application including ACCESS, WORD, and EXCEL, Lotus 123, Lotus Word Pro, WordPerfect Quattro Pro, Paradox, any communications, networking or groupware software, Lotus Notes, SQL database language

Mini computer based software skills

UNIX, 'C', Windows NT, 'C+ +'

Design methodologies

SSADM Version 4

Fig. 5. Skills most in demand and relatively cheap to learn.

Question time

Is it really possible to learn a new computing skill to a level sufficient to secure full-time work in the computer industry in just 6–12 months?

Yes it is, but it will not be easy. You will need access to the right training and the right tools and there is no substitute for very hard work. With this in mind, you will also learn fairly quickly whether a job in computing is a goal sufficiently important to you to warrant all the effort.

Learning 'in demand' computer skills

Learning practical, real, and in-demand computing skills in such a short period of time effectively rules out studying for the following types of qualifications:

- GCSEs
- 'A' levels
- university degrees
- other more longer term vocational and academic courses.

Even with most of the traditional academic and vocational qualifications ruled out, there are several methods available to you for learning your selected skills in the kind of timeframe envisaged.

Here are some of the most popular methods people in the computing industry use for acquiring technical skills in the shortest possible timeframe. Each will be discussed in greater length later in this chapter.

- Attending commercially run training courses.
- Attending college evening classes offering training in specific computer skills—like 'C/C++', Unix, Windows, Word, Excel, Visual Basic.
- Conducting a trial period of work with a local IT employer.

Hardware

Personal computers and components, PC networks and communications equipment, client/server technology, high performance CD ROM drives, high speed graphics cards, high speed modems, high resolution colour laser printers, high performance scanners, laptop and hand held computing devices, mobile telecommunications technology, computer sound systems, any multimedia hardware.

PC software skills

C++, Windows 95, Visual BASIC, any Microsoft Office application including ACCESS, WORD and EXCEL, Lotus 123, Lotus Word Pro, Paradox, any communications, networking or groupware software, Lotus Notes, SQL database language, any PC based relational or object oriented database, Borland's Delphi programming environment, any Internet access or security software Windows NT.

Minicomputer software skills

UNIX, INGRES, ORACLE, SYBASE, INFORMIX, SQL, RPG400, 'C/C++', COBOL, SAP, SYNON, AS400, Windows NT

Mainframe software skills

COBOL, DB/2, CICS

Design methodologies

SSADM Version 4, Prince

Fig. 6. Skills likely to be in demand over the next 2–3 years.

- Buying, renting, leasing or otherwise obtaining permanent access to a PC and, if appropriate, your selected software package(s). Then learning how to use it, program it, assemble and disassemble it, maintain it and repair it yourself—at home, school or some other convenient location.

- Consulting computer books, manuals, guides.

- Other methods.

Attending commercially run training courses

The best way to learn a new computing skill is first to have someone teach you how and then to practise it in a realistic environment. This is exactly what commercial training companies, specialising in the provision of training courses for specific software and hardware products, aim to do.

In addition:

- they aim to take the complete beginner to a reasonable level of proficiency in specific computing skills in around five days

- class sizes are small—a maximum of ten pupils and often only two or three

- all the required computer equipment and software is normally provided by the training company—at their own premises

- pupils can normally expect to have use of their own computer terminal.

At the end of the course, many training companies also give out published books and manuals on the subject all in addition to their own usually very detailed and voluminous course notes.

The major disadvantage with this kind of course is cost—often between £100 and £200 per day.

Learning new computer skills at college evening classes

A much less expensive but normally longer term method of learning key computing skills is to attend a relevant computing course at a local college. Most colleges now provide highly specific computer related courses on either a full time basis, or a two or three evenings a week basis, and sometimes even offer weekend courses.

Avoid courses like 'A' level computer science which tend to be academically biased. Look instead for courses likely to focus heavily on the skills you want to learn. Courses of this kind might include, for example:

- 'Unix in 10 weeks'
- 'C Programming'
- 'COBOL Programming'
- 'Introduction to Visual Basic for Windows 95'
- 'PC Assembly and Repair'

However, a short course such as:

- 'Introduction to Computers'
- 'Fundamentals of Computing'
- 'Computer Basics'

may be appropriate to begin with, depending on your current familiarity with computers.

Local college classes are likely to be:

- cheaper—typically costing less than £200 for the whole course
- available freely or at a substantial discount to those who qualify
- conveniently close to home
- shorter in duration—courses normally last between ten to 26 weeks
- larger—up to 40 pupils in some cases

- less well equipped—some students will have to share computing equipment and software.

Conducting a trial period of work with a local computer employer

Consider offering your services free, or at a nominal cost, to a local computer employer for a limited period of time. Do so on the understanding that in return for your free services, the employer will undertake to give you access to the computer equipment or software which you wish to learn and, better still, provide you with some in-house training too.

This approach, increasingly commonplace nowadays, can only be good for both parties. The employer has the benefit of your services at no charge and you get real experience and training in the computer skills you most want.

Buying your own PC and software

If none of the above methods is suitable for you, consider buying your own PC and, if appropriate, some software, and learning how to use it for yourself—in your own time. In fact you may consider investing in one anyway—it could well be useful later.

Reasonably equipped PCs can be bought these days for around £600 new—and a lot less for secondhand. Even with the appropriate software a PC will probably cost you a lot less than a single week's commercial training course.

Most of the software skills listed in Figure 5 can be learned by purchasing the appropriate additional software along with the PC. Software such as 'C/C++', VISUAL BASIC and most other PC software packages listed in Figure 5 can each be bought for around £300 and sometimes much less. Permanent access to both computer and software mean that you have all you require to start learning the skills you need.

For those interested in computer hardware, you need not buy the latest equipment. A collection of cheaper second hand computer components will be all you need to enable you to build, maintain and repair your own personal computer. By assembling parts and building your own computer you may even be able to make a profit by selling it at the end of your period of learning.

Consulting computer books, manuals and guides

By far the cheapest and most convenient method of learning new computer skills is from books. Recent surveys have shown that reading is the most popular method used by professionals already working in the computer industry to acquire new technical skills. It can be useful for newcomers too.

However, relying on reading alone to acquire new computing skills will not be sufficient for most newcomers to computing. Although reading will undoubtedly aid understanding of new and possibly complex subject areas, at the end of the day there really is no substitute for learning your computing skills using a keyboard and mouse, and sitting in front of a computer screen.

Using other methods of learning

There are several other less popular and arguably less effective methods for acquiring computing skills. They are listed here for completeness, but on their own they are unlikely to succeed in teaching you the new specific skills you will need to know. However, they can be of benefit if used alongside one or more other methods of learning. These include:

- videos instructing new users on specific software and hardware skills
- CAL (Computer Aided Learning) software
- TV programmes (especially those on some of the more specialised cable TV channels)
- correspondence courses.

Useful addresses

Videos and CAL software

The Software Warehouse, The Gyratory, Hangar Lane, London W5 1EE. Tel: (0181) 810 7770 or (01675) 466 467—for a range of video titles and CD-Rom based CAL software courses covering most of the popular PC based software packages.

Burgess Video Group, Unit 18, Industrial Estate, Brecon, Powys LD3 8LA. Tel: (01874) 611633; Fax: (01874) 622994—for a massive range (200+ titles).

Computer books and guides

Computer Manuals, Freepost, 205 Formans Road, Sparkhill, Birmingham B11 2BA. Tel: (0121) 706 6000; Fax: (0121) 706 3301 for a catalogue of hundreds of IT and computing specific books and manuals

Correspondence courses in computing

International Correspondence Schools (ICS), 8 Elliot Place, Clydeway Centre, Glasgow G3 8BR, Tel: (0141) 221 7373; Fax: (0141) 221 8151 for a range of programming courses in C and BASIC, Introduction to programming, and specialist hardware related courses on PC assembly, repair and maintenance.

Did you know . . . ?

1. If you want basic computer training, the chances are you will not have to pay for it. Most areas of the country are well served by government sponsored companies offering free computer training. Call in at your local Job Centre for details.
2. At any one point in time over 2,000 different computing skills are in demand in the computer job market.
3. The fastest growing sector of the computer job market is that for jobs specialising in personal computers and networks of smaller personal computers.

Question time

For which kinds of computing jobs are there the most vacancies?

By far the most common computing job vacancies are those for software developers, programmers, software engineers and support staff. Computer and software sales staff are also much in demand.

How long does it take to become fully familiar with a programming language such as 'C', 'C++' or VISUAL BASIC?

It depends whether you are learning and using these packages on a full time or part time basis, but in general expect it to take at least two to three months of fairly continuous use to get even reasonably proficient.

AIMING FOR A SPECIFIC JOB

The skills you have learned or have selected to learn should dictate the kind of computing job you eventually look for. Once skilled in, say, VISUAL BASIC or Windows 95 it is quite unlikely that you will be invited to an interview for a programming position using, say, COBOL. So aim at the kind of vacancies that specify your skill as being particularly required.

CASE STUDIES

Dave lists the help available to him

Dave diligently sets about considering what computing skills are most in demand in his local area. To do this he initially speaks to his school careers adviser who, as well as providing Dave with the names of a number of local computing employers and some useful information on the help available for school leavers looking for work, also suggests that Dave might visit his local library. There he finds a publication called the *Software Users Year Book* (see page 25) giving the names and addresses of thousands of computer related companies together with some of the hardware, software and services they use or supply.

Dave also lists some of the help and computer training that could be available if he needs it. Dave's list includes all of the Job Centres in his local area, the careers adviser he has already seen once, a local college evening class and, happily enough for Dave, his parents, who though not involved at all with computers, are more than willing and able to advise Dave objectively on his career ambitions.

Soon Dave comes to realise that for programming type positions —the ones he is most interested in—having the right programming skills is everything. Knowing PASCAL, for example, would be of no use at all to him if he were to apply for a vacancy that specified competency in VISUAL BASIC. After detailed market study of his own, Dave accurately assesses that his own skill areas—PCs, Windows 95 and VISUAL BASIC—are sufficiently in demand by local employers to give him a reasonable chance of finding work. Dave sets about further practising these programming skills on his own PC and again, through his local library, is able to borrow several books on VISUAL BASIC programming.

Jenny relies on her degree to secure her a job

Though perfectly aware of the help and advice her university careers adviser and local Job Centre can offer, Jenny, always independent and confident of her own ability to find work, sets about trying to prove that her university degree and her existing knowledge of computing issues will be sufficient on their own to find her the programming or systems analysis work she wants so much. Unfortunately, Jenny does not stop to consider what skills are in most demand in the computer job market and, although she is reasonably proficient in both the PASCAL and FORTRAN programming languages, she does not stop to consider that these skills, although popular a few years ago, are not greatly in demand nowadays.

However, Jenny does buy two books on systems analysis from which to learn. She also manages to get access to some CAL software that she can run on her own PC, which offers screen based tuition in a computer programming language called ADA—a language Jenny knows is widely used by companies working in the defence industry.

Even though her motives are sound, Jenny's approach to finding and learning the right computer skills is a little haphazard and lacks method. She has failed to realise that her best chances of finding programming or systems analysis work, even with her degree, is to research the computer skills market thoroughly and then to hone those skills she finds to be most in demand.

Steve wonders about training

Steve thinks carefully about the kind of help available from Job Centres and careers advisers for someone such as himself—already employed in a stable, reasonably good job and seemingly with little motivation to move on. He also begins to wonder how best to train himself for a new job, possibly in computer sales, computer training or maybe even in some kind of customer or user support role.

Steve instinctively knows that his existing insurance sales experience will probably be applicable to computer sales. However, he also knows that a more in-depth knowledge of computer systems, as well as some of the more popular software packages, is required if he is to have a realistic chance of finding a training or customer support type position.

Without a PC of his own and, with a mortgage and young family, unable to afford one either, Steve decides to enrol on a local evening college course offering tuition in four software packages: Excel—a spreadsheet program, Access—a database, Word—a popular word processor, and Powerpoint—a package for creating business graphics. Steve has heard that his own employers are just about to buy these packages for all of the PCs in his office and has read several computer magazines which appear to suggest these are popular packages used by both business and home users.

DISCUSSION POINTS

1. What computing skills do you feel are the ones most likely to be in demand for the computing jobs you have most in mind?

2. What steps can you take right now to ensure that you can acquire or can further practise the computing skills you have just identified?

3. What free help, advice and computer training will you be able to take advantage of to ensure success in your quest to find computing work?

4
Finding Computing Jobs

Armed with a job title or titles at which to aim, a list of potential IT employers and an idea of the help and free computer training available if the first wave of job applications fail, now is the time to start looking actively for computer jobs. There are several ways of doing this as this chapter will show.

READING THE ADVERTS

When companies place job advertisements, they normally do so with the aim of attracting as many interested job applicants as possible. This gives them the best possible selection from which to choose the successful candidate. Figure 7 shows some of the places computing job advertisements can be found.

Using local newspapers to find local work

Local newspapers, on the whole, tend to carry job advertisements placed by local companies. Therefore, if your job search area is restricted to your home town or surrounding districts, local newspapers are likely to prove much more fruitful than national newspapers.

The advertisement sections in local newspapers tend to be categorised for particular kinds of jobs. It is likely that most computing jobs will fall under a heading something like 'Professional and Technical' or simply 'Technical' rather than under 'Computing'. However, some larger advertisements could be placed elsewhere in the paper, so scan the whole paper rather than just the one section you feel is most appropriate.

In addition, most local newspapers advertise job vacancies on specific days of the week. You should therefore determine which day or days of the week your local newspapers advertise job vacancies—Thursdays are popular.

Sources of job advertisements

Computer recruitment agencies

Local, national and foreign newspapers

Specialised jobs newspapers

Careers offices at schools/universities

Channel 4 Teletext page 641

Computer trade magazines (like *Computing/Computer Weekly*)

Internet

Job Centres

Cable and occasionally regional television

National and local computer recruitment fairs

Fig. 7. Where UK companies advertise computing job vacancies.

Free 'pick me up' newspapers can also be a good source of local computing job vacancies. As they are free, pick up as many as you can. This kind of paper is often skimmed by readers and will often contain that precious job advertisement that many people overlook.

Reading national newspapers

National newspapers regularly carry advertisements for computer related job vacancies—again on certain days of the week only. Particular newspapers, like the ones listed below, regularly advertise computing jobs aimed primarily at graduates and higher level positions aimed at more experienced individuals.

National newspapers advertise national computing vacancies, so expect to find computing vacancies advertised in all areas of the country—even abroad in many cases.

Below is a list of national newspapers which one might expect to carry computing job vacancies and the days of the week on which computing vacancies are normally advertised at present.

Newspaper	Thursday	Saturday	Sunday
Daily Telegraph	x	x	x
The Times	x		x
The Guardian	x		

Consulting newspapers especially aimed at job hunters

Often published on a weekly basis, these papers *only* contain job advertisements, advice and other information likely to be of use to job seekers. They regularly carry articles relating to finding work in particular areas of industry—computing for example. Though general in nature, they are usually sectionalised by job category and often advertise all jobs in a related industry in one place, making computing or professional and technical vacancies much more easily accessible.

A recent survey of a single edition of *Jobs West*, a Bristol based weekly local jobs newspaper covering the South West area, and typical of newspapers of this kind, revealed that 22 different computer related job advertisements were placed, some advertising more than one position, made up as follows:

Position	*Quantity*
Trainee computer programmers	2
Computer programmers	7
Software engineers	3
Computer support/training	8
Operators	1
Hardware related	2
Computer/software sales and marketing	5
Totals	28*

**For the purposes of this sample, it was assumed that advertisements appearing to specify that more than one position was available within the same company were in fact offering two identical positions.*

Of the 22 different advertisements:

- Only one mentioned academic qualifications at all. This advert was for a 'junior software engineer' and specified 'A' level standard qualifications were required.

- Twelve appeared to insist on previous computing or software experience.

- Five mentioned that full training would be given to suitable candidates.

- Six indicated that an active interest in computing, software, hardware or other computing specific areas was of most importance.

- As expected, all 22 advertisements were for jobs located within a 30 mile radius of Bristol.

- Predictably, salaries varied greatly between £7,000 and £35,000. Three positions were also advertised as offering company cars to the successful applicants.

- All intended to interview prospective candidates, though none mentioned computer aptitude tests at all.

USING THE COMPUTER TRADE PRESS

The computer industry is well served with trade specific journals, publications, newspapers and magazines. Many concentrate specifically on computing, providing information, articles and job advertisements aimed directly at those already employed within the industry and those considering a move into computers for the first time.

Trade publications such as *Computer Weekly* and *Computing*, both weekly 'glossy newspapers', are commonly available free (on application) to individuals already working in the computer industry. For computing job seekers not yet part of the industry, both papers cost around £1.50–£1.75 per issue at the time of writing, and can be purchased or ordered from most major newsagents.

Computing, VNU Business Publications, VNU House, 32–34 Broadwick Street, London W1A 2HG. Tel: (0171) 316 9000; Fax: (0171) 316 9160.

Computer Weekly, Reed Business Publishing, Quadrant House, The Quadrant, Sutton, Surrey SM2 5AS. Tel: (01444) 441212; Fax: (01444) 445588.

Computing jobs in all areas of the country

These two publications contain details of a massive range of computing jobs covering all areas of the computer industry.

Although aimed primarily at existing computer professionals, these publications also carry advertisements designed to attract **interested novices** with suitable practical skills—even if they have been self taught. Many adverts are placed by computer recruitment agencies—specialist job agencies appointed by computing companies to act on their behalf, though many are also placed directly by employers themselves.

Both publications also carry a healthy spread of both UK wide and overseas computing vacancies.

Specialised publications

Although both *Computer Weekly* and *Computing* deal primarily with the computer industry, several other publications specialise even further, concentrating on particular areas of computing such as those connected with personal computers, communications, networking and minicomputers. Magazines such as *PC Week* carry all sorts of useful information and many job advertisements geared primarily to attract staff specialising in the programming, maintenance and use of personal computers.

PC Week, VNU Business Publications, VNU House, 32–34 Broadwick Street, London W1A 2HG. Tel: (0171) 316 9000; Fax: (0171) 316 9160.

Network Computing, Business and Technical Communications, 24 High St, Beckenham, Kent BR3 1AY. Tel: (0181) 663 3818.

Unix Systems, Eaglehead Publishing, Maybury Road, Woking, Surrey GU21 5HX. Tel: (01483) 740271.

Studying advertising levels in trade magazines

A short study of the two main computer trade publications, *Computer Weekly* and *Computing*, revealed that both papers have an average of around 50–60 pages of jobs in a single issue—with some individual pages advertising in excess of 50 positions. Overall each publication probably carries more than 1,500 separate vacancies in each issue!

From these figures it can clearly be seen that applying for a free subscription, or even purchasing if necessary a few issues of these trade newspapers, will be extremely worth while. Although many computing vacancies will be for positions located in the South East and around major cities, coverage is nationwide—including Scotland, Wales, Northern and Southern Ireland. The USA, Australia, New Zealand and most European countries are also served well.

Again academic levels of achievement are seldom mentioned—except for overseas jobs. Previous demonstrable experience, interest and aptitude count for much more.

USING TELEVISION, RADIO AND ON-LINE SERVICES

A surprising number of computing vacancies are now being broadcast on TV and radio. Mainstream TV information providers such as Teletext regularly update their pages with their customers' lists of advertised computing vacancies. At the time of writing page 641 of Channel 4's Teletext service carried around 25 pages of computing jobs—around 250 different job vacancies in all—many specifying that more than one person was required.

These advertisements comprised on average

- 84 positions for programmers, software engineers and software developers
- 50 positions for staff in customer/user support roles
- 20 positions for hardware related work such as design, maintenance and repair
- 28 positions for computer operators
- 68 assorted other positions including those for systems analysts, project or team leaders, computer trainers, and salespeople.

For those who have a cable television service, several channels broadcast computing job vacancies between programmes. Often placed by local employment agencies, these positions are usually only very briefly described. Details such as job title, geographic location and salary are given together with a telephone or other contact number for you to ring if you are interested.

Listening to the radio

Local (commercial) radio stations often broadcast details of local computing vacancies. Though these are broadcast along with jobs in other industry areas, more information is generally given about details such as the employer, nature of the position, salary and the kind of person the company is looking for.

Did you know . . . ?

1. It is said that only 10 per cent of all computing jobs get advertised. The remaining 90 per cent of available posts get filled before advertisements are even placed.
2. Though employers might not currently be advertising or looking for new staff, a quality speculative letter describing yourself, your skills, experience and interests will occasionally lead potential employers to consider 'finding a position for you' and hiring you anyway.

3. With many candidates of similar academic ability and experience applying for computing job vacancies, employers often choose the candidate with the neatest handwriting or the most interesting hobbies or some other positive, distinguishing attribute.

Question time

I am a quite experienced user of some of the popular PC software packages. How can I find the largest numbers of computing job vacancies in the shortest period of time?

If you are willing to work anywhere in the UK then apply for a free subscription to *Computing* or *Computer Weekly*. If you want to focus your efforts on finding local work, then buy a couple of specialised, local job seekers' newspapers and also your local newspaper on the day of the week job vacancies are mainly advertised. Also regularly visit your local Job Centre and contact a few of your local computer recruitment agencies—you will find them listed in the *Yellow Pages* under 'Employment Agencies'.

I am not at all experienced with computers but I am interested in working with them on a part or full time basis. Do I have any real chance of securing computer related work immediately?

You may have some chance of securing work in computer or software sales. You may even be lucky enough to secure other types of work such as a VDU operator or even some kinds of computer and users support roles. However, realistically you would do best to invest some time, and perhaps a little money if necessary, in obtaining some computer training before applying for other kinds of computing jobs. See chapter 3 for further details.

Using other on-line services

Some computing magazines and trade journals, particularly those catering for freelance and temporary computer staff, are offering a job advertising service for their readers on the **Internet**. As the popularity of this medium grows rapidly, so will the number of computing jobs advertised on it. The following is a short list of computer related publications together with their Internet or bulletin board addresses.

Publication	Internet Address
Computing	http://www.vnu.co.uk/bc/ctg

Computer Contractor	http://www.vnu.co.uk/vnu/cc
Freelance Informer	on line bulletin board service available to computer and modem owners. Tel: 0181 652 3444 (28800 bps).

APPROACHING EMPLOYERS DIRECTLY

Since only around one in ten of all computing vacancies ever reach the stage where they get advertised, it is important to understand how the other 90 per cent are filled and to seek ways of turning this information to your advantage.

Block advertisements in newspapers, jobs newspapers and trade magazines often attract literally hundreds of applicants. Whilst replying to published advertisements in your search for computing work is a perfectly normal and necessary method of operation, you will have a better chance of success by making a concerted effort to find vacancies that have yet to be advertised. By doing this you will greatly increase the probability that:

- you will be one of perhaps only a select few applicants to have applied for the job—in some cases you may be the only applicant

- you fill the vacancy without it ever being advertised.

From the statistic you can see that this must happen a lot—but how?

There are several methods. Computer recruitment agencies (fully discussed in chapter 6) often place people with computing companies long before they have to advertise the position. However, many other methods exist for finding and filling unadvertised job vacancies in the computing field. Here are some of them.

Writing to companies

Writing speculative letters to employers inquiring whether or not any existing job vacancies exist can be a fruitful method of finding **unadvertised work**. A simple letter of enquiry, accompanied by a brief summary of your personal skills and experience or prefferably a copy of your CV, should be enough to prompt many employers into at least contacting you if and when vacancies materialise.

8 Treetop Close,
Lower Westbury,
London SW1 1QW
Tel: (0171) 123 4567
19 September 199X

Mrs Janet Simpson,
Personnel Manager,
Real Time Scientific Software Ltd,
11 Employer Road,
London SW1 5FD

Dear Mrs Simpson,

I am writing to enquire whether you have any vacancies in your computer department at present—preferably as a junior software engineer or trainee computer programmer.

A word about myself. I am 18 and have just left sixth form college with two 'A' levels, one in Computer Science (grade 'A'), and five GCSEs.

I am keen on sports—I played on the wing for the school's rugby team, but my real interest is programming computers. I used my own Intel 486 PC to write my Computer Science 'A' level project software (a program written in 'C' and some assembler which calculates planetary orbits). Also using 'C', I have written a small but fully functional chess program and, using Visual Basic, my last project was to write a Windows 95 based program which solved elementary mathematical equations.

All in all I have around 18 months' experience of writing PC based software using Microsoft's 'C/C++' compiler, the MASM assembler and Visual Basic, and knowing of your company's fine reputation for producing real time software, yours is the kind of company I would most like to work for.

I have enclosed a copy of my CV which details some of the other software packages I am familiar with and slightly more detail for each of the home and school based projects I have undertaken so far.

I am immediately available to attend an interview and could, if requested, be available to start work within two weeks. I look forward to hearing from you soon.

Yours sincerely,

Alan Briggs

Fig. 8. Sample speculative letter to a potential employer of computer programmers.

Use your list of potential employers for name and address details.

A model speculative letter aimed at stimulating employer interest in employing a trainee computer programmer is given at figure 8 and one aimed at securing a job maintaining and repairing computer hardware is given at figure 9.

Getting into the habit

Realistically your chances of instant success with a single speculative letter are small. However, your chances will be significantly increased by writing one or two letters regularly—every day if possible. If you can manage, say, two letters every day for a week then in theory you will have increased your chances of a favourable response 14 fold. An on-going policy of writing, say, one or two letters per day may well eventually lead to your first computing job. However, it is important to remember that quantity alone will not ensure success. Quality is every bit as important and more so. Quality in this respect means:

- quality of **stationery**—envelopes, paper and so on
- using best **handwriting** or preferably laser printed or typed letters
- enclosing full personal information (a **CV**), a clear indication of the kind of position sought, your availability for work or an interview, your main qualifications, computing skills and level of experience. Remember to also include a telephone number and state when you may be contacted
- addressing the letter to a **named person** if possible, rather than simply 'The Personnel Manager'
- always sending correspondence by **first class post**—using second class postage risks employers thinking that either you do not attach much importance to your applications, or that you have posted hundreds of similar letters and are merely trying to cut costs
- enclosing an **SAE** for the employer's reply.

8 Treetop Close,
Lower Westbury,
London SW1 1QW.
Tel: (0171) 123 4567
19 September 199X

Mr James Lewis,
Personnel Manager,
Computer Hardware Maintenence Ltd,
12 Employer Road,
London SW1 5FX.

Dear Mr Lewis,

I am writing to enquire whether you have any vacancies in your computer maintenance and repair section.

A word about myself. I am 16 and have just left school with four GCSE qualifications, including maths and physics, and I intend to further my studies by attending an evening class in electronics with my local college.

I am keen on cycling and flying my home built model aeroplanes, but ever since being asked by a friend to help build a computer system from scratch, my main interest has been for building, maintaining and repairing computers. To date I have built five personal computers from scratch, regularly service and maintain three Hewlett Packard laser printers and a Canon photocopier for my father's own business, and have successfully disassembled, repaired and reassembled a number of older computers such as the Commodore 64 and Atari ST for friends and relatives.

All in all I have over three years' practical experience of building and maintaining computer and other office equipment. This includes identifying the new parts required, sourcing and buying the relevant electronic components, disassembling the equipment, fitting and testing these components and finally reassembling the equipment and ensuring it is fully functional before finishing.

I have enclosed a copy of my CV which describes some of the above 'projects' in more detail. Should I be considered suitable, I am immediately available to attend interview and could, if requested, be available to start work within two weeks. I look forward to hearing from you soon.

Yours sincerely,

David Noble

Fig. 9. Sample speculative letter to a potential employer of computer maintenance and repair staff.

Remember to keep copies of all letters sent and to record on your list of potential employers that a letter has been sent and the date it was posted. As replies begin to arrive through your letter box, remember to update your list accordingly.

Telephoning and visiting potential employers

The personnel sections of computing companies and individual computing project managers are no different from any other staff recruiters. Their needs are just as urgent and their budgets are equally constrained. Anything which is perceived by them as making their jobs easier will be both welcomed and well rewarded.

So consider removing the need for personnel managers and project leaders to read your entire letter. Why not telephone and ask directly whether any vacancies exist for computer related work? Ask for the person in charge of computer recruitment, or preferably for a named person. If that person is not available, simply leave a message and your contact number or find out the best time to call back.

Visiting employers' premises is a method much less often tried. There are distinct disadvantages in doing so. However, if you manage to get a hearing, perhaps having telephoned earlier to arrange a convenient time for your visit, you will in effect have invited yourself for an interview, albeit an informal one.

ADVERTISING YOURSELF

If you have been unable to find advertised vacancies and your speculative letters have failed to elicit any favourable response, consider some form of **self advertising**. Advertising yourself means using any acceptable method of highlighting yourself, your skills and your previous experience to potential employers. This includes placing 'wanted' advertisements in the recruitment sections of newspapers, trade journals and job hunting papers, but stops short of other methods like posting adverts in shop windows or on car windscreens. These latter methods are of doubtful value and the potential risks associated with attracting unsolicited and unwanted enquiries normally outweigh the benefits of this form of personal advertising.

CASE STUDIES

Dave learns an early lesson

Because he wants local work Dave plans to start visiting his local Job Centre on a daily basis. He asks the staff there which days most vacancies on display are updated, and resolves to attend at times immediately after fresh new vacancies are displayed.

He also starts to pick up free newspapers. These provide him with a number of new leads. He also purchases a local, more specialised, weekly job hunting newspaper costing a mere 70 pence and one trade journal, *Computing*, every week for £1.75.

Dave does not initially like the thought of telephoning employers directly and so resolves to write at least one speculative letter per day to local computing companies taken from his potential employers list. However, by not keeping copies or updating his list of potential employers Dave does cause some confusion with a couple of employers who receive duplicated letters of enquiry. As a result of this, Dave hears no more from them, but at least he has learned early on that meticulous preparation and record keeping are essential to avoid losing potential opportunities.

Jenny actively seeks nationally advertised computing vacancies

Prepared to work anywhere in the UK, Jenny does not intend to read local newspapers or local job hunting papers. Armed with a copy of several Sunday quality newspapers, a free subscription to two leading computer trade journals and a fortnightly copy of *The Graduate Post*—a publication advertising job vacancies particularly suitable for graduates—she soon builds up a list of companies to which she can apply for work. Declining the services of university careers advisers and local Job Centres and preferring to go it alone in her search for work, Jenny considers that having a degree level qualification should probably ensure some kind of computing job so long as she continues to search for and regularly apply for work.

Steve thinks the time is right for a career change

After ten years with the same insurance company and with a good reputation there, Steve feels that, though the time is right for a change in his career, he can remain in his current job until he finds exactly the computer related job he wants. He will prepare carefully, research the computer job market, and seek out as many different advertisements and opportunities as possible. To do this, he starts visiting his local Job Centre in his lunch hour. He particularly notices the high numbers of computer sales and marketing type positions advertised there. He observes that most of these types of position seem to offer commission based salaries. With a family and mortgage, Steve feels that these types of position might be a little risky.

Steve also makes a point of buying the local evening paper every Thursday—a day of the week widely used in the newspaper industry for advertising computing jobs. Two local free newspapers are already delivered to his home every Friday. Still, Steve thinks that more can be done. His commercial skills and wealth of previous experience are his main selling points and Steve begins to consider whether he should write all these up into a fully fledged CV, which he could then distribute to a few computer recruitment agencies as well as some local employers. A good idea. Steve has not written a CV before and has certainly never contacted specialised recruitment agencies, and so resolves to do a little more research on both, rather than risk acting in haste.

Steve is also beginning to feel that a job in computer training or computer sales are the only types of job he is interested in.

DISCUSSION POINTS

1. How do you intend to make yourself aware of as many advertised computer related job vacancies as possible?

2. Given that most computing vacancies are filled before they are even advertised, how do you intend to make sure you become aware of as many unadvertised IT job vacancies as possible?

3. How many speculative letters do you intend to write to IT employers each week and how will you ensure that you keep track of which companies you have written to and the responses they make?

5
Writing a Hard Hitting CV

What is a CV?

A CV, short for 'Curriculum Vitae'—a Latin phrase meaning literally 'schedule of life', is simply a written personal history of an individual. It is primarily designed to give its recipients —usually employers—a reasonably short, hard hitting summary of an individual's, education, work experience, sporting achievements, interests and skills, together with other more personal details like name, address, contact telephone numbers and so on.

In the IT world, a CV should be complete with enough detail for a recruiting employer to decide there and then whether to invite its subject for interview.

PREPARING A CV

Since most IT employers request a copy of your CV early on in their recruitment process—certainly before an interview—you should start thinking of preparing one as soon as possible, preferably before you start applying for computing vacancies.

Preparing a CV involves producing either a small document or even a single sheet of paper, containing your personal details and all of the skills and experience that you think will be applicable to your future job applications. A model CV is shown in Figure 11.

Although there are no hard and fast rules for how CVs should be presented to IT employers, there are several schools of thought on the subject. One says that your CV should be contained on one side of a single sheet of A4 sized paper. Easy to handle, hard hitting, and as brief but relevant as possible, a single sheet will make the employer's task of reading and assessing you much easier than it would be for someone who presents a ten page, detailed CV.

Another suggests that a CV should contain a summary of your main personal details, skills and experience on the first page, followed by a more in depth treatment of your personal, educational and employment history on between one and three subsequent pages. In this way, if the employer is interested enough to want more detailed information after reading your front page, then it is immediately available.

A third school of thought dictates that the CV is so important when applying for computer related work that it really ought to be prepared on your behalf by one of the many professional companies that undertake such work. The expense involved in doing this will be more than compensated for by the extra employer interest that is almost bound to result.

There is something to be learned from all these approaches. How you prepare your own CV will probably depend on whether you are still at school, university, or already have full time work.

What your CV is selling

Your CV should sell **you**, your computing and other **skills** and your **experience** to employers. With particular job vacancies in mind, it should tell employers what they want to hear.

Let us look at the situation from the employers' viewpoint. Imagine yourself as a personnel manager in the computing department of a large company. A project manager is continually pressing you to find quality staff to fill three different vacancies—all as trainee computer programmers. You have no one on file who seems applicable and you have therefore placed an advertisement in the local newspaper. You are inundated with 300 replies. What do you do?

With CVs of an average of four or five sheets of paper accompanying each application, you have nearly 1,500 sheets of paper to read, some of which have information written on both sides. Assuming you intend to interview a short list of twelve candidates for the three positions, you are immediately faced with having to discard 288 of the 300 applications.

Although you will want to look at every application, human nature and time pressure will dictate that, for most of the time, you will be looking for excuses to add to the discard pile. Your excuses will include:

- untidy, handwritten presentation and poor grammar and spelling

- evidence that the application has been prepared hastily, thoughtlessly or otherwise unsuitably

- evidence that the application has been photocopied or is so general in nature as to be suitable for almost any computing job, rather than the particular vacancies you have advertised

- evidence that the candidate has misunderstood the nature of the job being applied for

- failure by the applicant to supply a CV, or all of the documentation or information requested in the advertisement, or submission in a form other than that specified in the advertisement

- the applicant has forwarded a multi-paged, voluminous application, far too large and unwieldy to read in the timescales you need to work within

- poor overall quality of the application, including poor stationery and poor presentation

- the application was received after the deadline date specified in the advertisement.

Following this sifting procedure, you may be surprised to find that over 250 applications can immediately be discarded. The amount of time you actually spend looking at each individual application might be extremely short—just a few seconds in some cases, before you quickly dispatch them to the rapidly growing discard pile.

You will only spend more time than this on quality applications —those that **demand your attention**, those that have been submitted in the form asked for, on time and attractively.

Fifty applicants make it through to your second vetting stage. Your next task is to select twelve of the best applicants from the 50, and preferably to telephone or possibly write to them to arrange interviews in just a few days time. You decide that, in order to achieve your interview short list of twelve, more stringent selection criteria must now be applied.

You, in line with many IT personnel managers, decide that the two most important requirements of the remaining applicants are:

- the applicant's computing skills, knowledge, experience and interests

- the applicant's availability for work.

All of the 50 remaining applicants have enclosed a CV of between one and four pages in length, on quality stationery, and well presented in either typed or laser printed form. Everything about them indicates the professionalism with which they have been prepared and presented. All candidates look potentially suitable for interview. But you must select twelve—and quickly.

Since your posts need to be filled ideally within four weeks, sooner if possible, you sensibly decide that any applicant who is unable to become available within four weeks can be excluded (20 in all).

Skills and experience are considered surprisingly late on in the vetting process. All applicants have displayed some evidence of computer related interest, skills and experience. You decide, as many personnel managers do for trainee programmer vacancies, that evidence of enthusiasm, home computing projects and some evidence of previous programming experience are more important than academic achievement. With this in mind, you are naturally interested to confirm that applicants have had at least a reasonable standard of education—preferably in computer, English or mathematical type subjects.

The key selection criteria

Following the course taken by many IT personnel managers before you, you decide that the following criteria will be used to select the twelve interview candidates:

- preference will be given to those with previous programming experience of any kind and however acquired

- strong preference will be given to applicants who have specifically mentioned the programming language or other software tools or computer equipment to be used on the computer project for which you are recruiting

- strong preference will be given to applicants who have demonstrated evidence of an active interest in writing computer software—perhaps by writing programs in their own time, at home or after school or college

- everything else being equal, preference will also be given to applicants who 'have gone the extra mile' in their effort to find work or who have otherwise distinguished their applications in some way from all the others.

Learning some lessons

As the personnel manager, you have come a long way since first placing the original job advertisement. From 300 original candidates you sensibly applied a number of commonly used procedures to reduce the number of interviewees to just twelve.

Now put on your job seeker's hat again. Some valuable lessons can be learned from this experience, all of which you can apply to ensure that your application and CV are prepared meticulously, correctly and that together, they ensure that you reach personnel managers' interview short lists.

The lessons are:

- excellent, well presented CVs get you interviews

- shoddy or hasty presentation leads to failure very quickly

- CVs should be between one and a maximum of four pages in length, typed, or better still laser printed, on quality bond weight paper

- the information you give in your CV should be easily accessible and presented attractively

- all relevant personal details including important telephone and other contact details should be clearly presented on your CV, together with details of all your computer related skills of any kind

Name	Alan Briggs
Date of birth	16 August 1979.
Software used	WordPerfect for Windows, DBASE 5, Limited knowledge of Corel Draw, Lotus 123, Some Unix. C/C++, Visual Basic
Hardware used	Personal computers.
Notice period	About two weeks.
School education	Highworth Sixth Form College, Rush Hill, London SW19 2LE
Academic Results	GCSEs— Computing 'B', French 'C', Physics 'C', Maths 'B', English 'C', Geography 'E', Chemistry 'E', A Levels—Computing 'A', Maths 'C', Physics 'F'

Other information

I am currently taking an evening class at Highfield College.
I am a member of the Highworth Chess Club.

Fig. 10. Extract from a badly-written CV.

- to make it easier for employers to spot particularly relevant skills such as competence in particular types of hardware or software, such skills should be **emboldened**, underlined or *otherwise emphasised.*

SELLING YOURSELF TO EMPLOYERS IN THE COMPUTER INDUSTRY

In the computer industry, perhaps more than most industry areas, your CV **sells** you. The quality of your CV and the skills and experience listed on it will be directly proportional to the number of interviews you get invited to.

Therefore, no matter how long it takes, your CV must be meticulously prepared, drafted, redrafted, polished and produced, so that the final result is as perfect as you can make it.

Your CV has to make employers feel that you are the right person for the job. Everything about it must reek of quality. Every last relevant detail, skill and morsel of experience must be included.

MAKING THE MOST OF YOUR COMPUTING SKILLS

Consider the two CV extracts in Figures 10 and 11. Both describe the same person with the same skills. Which one would you be most impressed with as an employer?

The full version of Alan Briggs' CV is shown in Figure 12 later in this chapter.

Tips for making the most of your background, skills and experience

1. If you are **single** then say so—in bold print. Many computing jobs involve lots of travel, and sometimes prolonged stays at customers' sites. Rightly or wrongly, IT employers regard single people as being more mobile and therefore more suitable.
2. If you **own a car**, or hold a full, valid or clean UK driving licence, then make this clear on your CV. Owning or being able to drive a car is a prerequisite for many kinds of computing jobs—particularly in computer and software sales, support, training, and hardware installation, maintenance and repair.
3. Highlight, **in bold print**, ALL of the relevant software or hardware products you have used or have any **experience** of. For hardware, always specify manufacturer names and where

Name	**Alan Briggs**	
Date of birth	16 August 1979.	
Marital status	**Single, no children**.	
Car owner	Yes, full, clean driving licence.	
Interests	Chess, rugby, music, travel.	
		Experience
Main computer skills	**Microsoft Visual 'C/C++' 2.0**	18 months
	Microsoft MASM Version 6	18 months
	Windows 3.1/Windows 95	2 years
	MS-DOS Version 6.22	2 years
	Visual BASIC Version 4	12 months
	IBM Personal computers	24 months
	IBM RS/6000 (running Unix)	3 months
Other software used	**WordPerfect for Windows Version 6, DBASE 5, Corel Draw Version 6 Lotus 123 Version 4.0, Aix Version 3.21, Microsoft Excel 5.0, Word 6.0, Access 2.0**	
Availability	**Two weeks notice** (at most).	
School education	Highworth Sixth Form College, Rush Hill, London SW19 2LE	
Academic results	5 GCSEs—Computing 'B', French 'C', Physics 'C', Maths 'B', English 'C'. 2 A Levels—Computing 'A', Maths 'C'	

Other information

I am currently taking a college evening class at Highfield College in '**Unix Programming**'.

Last Christmas I took a temporary job for two weeks at the Post Office delivering mail.

I am a member of the Highworth Chess Club and regularly play league and tournament chess.

Fig. 11. Extract from a well-written CV.

possible model numbers. For software, always specify the latest version number of the software used. This will give potential employers a far more concrete idea of the computer technology you are familiar with. Quoting the latest versions/models of the software/hardware you have used will convince employers that your technical skills and experience are also current.

4. For each of the hardware and software products you have listed, specify **how much experience** you have had with it, in terms of years and months—providing you have at least one month's experience of it. List the names, versions or models only of computer products you have less than a month's experience of. IT employers are very interested in the length of time (experience) you have had to become familiar with and to practise using certain software packages—even if this experience has been gained at home.
5. If you can be available at **four weeks' notice** or less, then make a point of emphasising this. Employers in the computer industry needing to fill vacant positions urgently (which is most of them), tend to prefer and recruit candidates whose notice periods are relatively short, often over candidates with otherwise superior technical skills.
6. If you **use a computer** at home, school, college, university or at work, then always describe its model number, manufacturer, details of the software used on it and what your responsibilities and interests are in connection with it.
7. Only list academic, vocational and professional **qualifications** that you passed at an acceptable grade.
8. If you are **studying** a computer related subject in your spare time then make sure you include details of this. In addition, always list any commercial (non-academic) computer training courses you have attended. This will convince IT employers that you have been professionally trained in your subject and, importantly, that they will not have to bear the cost of such training themselves. Yes—it is a harsh world out there.
9. Do not forget to list your **major personal achievements** too. These might include sporting achievements, other academic achievements, successful or otherwise relevant work experience and anything else you can think of that will cause an employer to perceive you in a good light.

TAILORING YOUR CV

Tailoring your CV means altering, or producing a slightly revised copy of, your 'standard' CV in order to make it particularly relevant or applicable to a job vacancy for which you intend to apply.

With the large number of different types of computing jobs available, it is reasonable to assume that most individuals will be suited to more than one or two. In these cases, it is perfectly acceptable for you to produce a modified version of your CV which more strongly emphasises the particular skills and experience you feel will be of most interest to employers with specific types of vacancy.

It is perfectly normal and moral for job applicants to make the very most of their applicable computer skills and knowledge. If this means placing different emphasis on different skills for different job vacancies, then this is perfectly acceptable—indeed necessary. The extra time and effort required to prepare a 'customised' CV is normally well worth the effort.

Do not be tempted, however, to make fictitious claims about the extent of your experience. You will be found out sooner or later.

Did you know . . . ?

1. Many employers decide whether to interview or reject an applicant based solely on a very cursory glance at the front page of his or her CV.
2. Employers do not normally read through every last detail on a CV—they do not have time. The onus is firmly on job applicants to produce CVs which **demand** to be read further.
3. CVs longer than five pages may not get read at all.

Question time

Is there anywhere I can go to get help in preparing my CV?

Yes. Depending on your personal circumstances you might consider availing yourself of the services of

- your local Job Centre (free)
- a computer recruitment agency (normally free)
- a professional CV writing company (around £40 minimum).

Should I include on my CV the names and addresses of people who have agreed to supply personal references for me?
The debate on whether to include referees on your CV rages on. However, consider **not** including them to begin with. Employers generally ask for personal references *after* an interview has taken place. They may also make any job offer conditional on receiving satisfactory references and most computer recruitment agencies do not specifically ask for them straight away.

Have you got any other tips on writing computer oriented CVs?

- Always use white, A4 paper. If laser printed, use at least 12 point fonts. If typed, ensure the ribbon you use is new and the print quality high.

- Always use standard, well known product names and not abbreviations. For example, use VISUAL BASIC version 4.0 rather than VB4.

- Do not make your CV gimmicky by using too many fancy fonts or italics.

- If possible distribute your CV in an A4 sized envelope and avoid folding and stapling your CV. Always send CVs, especially to employers, by first class mail.

- A model CV, that of a school leaver wanting to secure work as a trainee computer programmer, is shown in Figure 12.

DISTRIBUTING YOUR CV

Once prepared, your CV now has to be effectively distributed. This will certainly mean making several if not many copies of it. If you have access to a laser printer or photocopying machine, this will be all you need to produce multiple copies of your CV reasonably cheaply. If not then a private printing or photocopying service will do the job at reasonable rates if you shop around and, for some, the local Job Centre provides such facilities.

CURRICULUM VITAE ALAN BRIGGS SEPT 1997

PERSONAL DETAILS

Home address	8 Treetop Close, Lower Westbury, London SW1 1QW. United Kingdom. Tel: (0171) 123 4567	
Date of birth	16 August 1979.	
Nationality	British.	
Marital status	**Single, no children.**	
Disabilities	None.	
Car owner	Yes, full, clean driving licence.	
Interests	Chess, rugby, music, travel.	
		Experience
Main computer skills	**Microsoft Visual 'C/C++'**	18 months
	Microsoft MASM Version 6	18 months
	Windows 3.1/Windows 85	2 years
	MS-DOS Version 6.	2 years
	Visual BASIC Version 4	12 months
	Personal computers	24 months
	Minicomputers (running Unix)	3 months
Other software used	**WordPerfect for Windows, DBASE 5, Corel Draw Lotus 123, Unix, Microsoft Excel, Word, Access.**	
Availability	**Two weeks' notice** (at most).	
School education	Highworth Sixth Form College, Rush Hill, London. Tel: 0171 123458.	
Academic results	5 GCSEs—Computing 'B', French 'C', Physics 'C', Maths 'B', English 'C'. 2 A Levels—Computing 'A', Maths 'C'.	

Other information

I am currently taking a college evening class at Highfield College in '**Unix Programming**'.

Last Christmas I took a temporary job for two weeks at the Post Office delivering mail.

I am a member of the Highworth Chess Club.

Details of home and school based computer projects

'A' level project. 'Planetary Orbits'. Written in **Microsoft 'C/C++' Version 2** and **Assembler**. Learning these skills along the way, I used my home computer (**an IBM Pentium PC**) to write a computer program which plotted, in graphical form, the orbits of the nine planets in our solar system. This involved simulating a graphical model of the sun in the centre of the computer screen with the planets rotating around it at a speed and orbit consistent with those actually seen and recorded by astronomers. Although I am not an astronomer, I found it fascinating to model planetary data, gleaned from a book in the school library, on the computer. I used **'C'** for most of the calculations and **Microsoft MASM Assembler Version 6** for the moving graphics.

Home Project 1. 'SmallChess'. Written entirely in **'C'** on **Microsoft Windows 95**, I have produced a small but functional chess program, which I wanted to use to practise with. The program displays a fairly basic graphical representation of the board and pieces and two clocks showing how much time the computer and human player have left to make their moves. After almost three months of development, mainly in the evenings, the program is now playing recognisable, albeit weak, chess. It was a great thrill for me when the program completed its first whole game of chess.

Home Project 2. My old maths teacher at Highfield School asked me to produce a program which solves elementary equations to be used to teach some of the students the various methods by which this can be achieved. To do this I chose to learn and write the program in **VISUAL BASIC 4.0**. The result was an attractive **Windows 95** program which is now in use at Highfield School.

Fig. 12. An example of a full CV geared to finding computing jobs.

How many copies will you need?

If you are responding to job advertisements, contacting recruitment agencies or writing speculative letters to IT employers on a daily or even a weekly basis, then clearly you will need a good stock of CVs. Most correspondence in such instances will demand that a CV accompanies the application, covering or speculative letter.

Computer related employers rarely consider speculative enquiries or job applications that are not accompanied by a full CV. Recruitment agencies without exception require at least one copy of a CV before they begin to act on your behalf.

Normally, a stock of around five to 20 copies should suffice, depending on the regularity and effectiveness of your job search programme.

CASE STUDIES

Dave makes the most of his home computing experience

Dave, aiming primarily at trainee computer programming positions, produces a single version of his CV to accompany both his job applications and his speculative letters. Keen to emphasise his strengths and to underplay his lack of academic qualifications, Dave redrafts his CV four times and spends a total of nearly 20 hours paying attention to detail and ensuring that all his relevant skills and experience are included. By the time his marathon effort has been completed, Dave has managed to produce a fine looking CV. At first sight his CV appeared to be that of a highly experienced, enthusiastic and motivated individual, rather than of the school leaver with an interest in computers that he was in reality.

Dave has carefully selected facts and highlighted particularly useful phrases and words such as the manufacturer of his home computer and the name of the programming languages and software packages he has used.

As a school leaver, Dave also emphasises the fact that he is immediately available for both interviews and any work that is offered.

After applying for several positions and after having dispatched around 15 CVs with speculative letters to local employers, Dave finds that the quality of his CV leads three companies to respond with offers of job interviews. Two of these are for trainee programming positions and one is for a job as a 'junior software engineer'.

One of the employers asks Dave to bring along samples of the programming work he has completed in his spare time. After initial hesitation, Dave decides that a few printed program listings could be tidied up and presented at all three interviews as evidence of his past work. This would, if nothing else, present companies with concrete proof of his current ability.

He also decides that, even if it could not be used, he will also take a floppy disk along, containing some of his programs. He also thinks that it would do no harm at all to take along some of the photographs he has taken of his computer screen whilst it was running his software. At the very least, Dave thinks, this might distinguish his application from all the others, in the minds of the interview panel.

Jenny emphasises her degree level qualifications

Jenny uses her own computer and printer to produce her CV. Although she knows that academic qualifications are of secondary importance to many IT employers, she feels that there must be something in the fact that around half of all available new computing jobs are filled by graduates.

With this in mind Jenny prepares a CV emphasising her forthcoming degree level qualification and giving only brief details of some of the practical experience she has gained on the course. So keen is she to make the most of her academic achievement that she completely omits to detail the fact that she owns a computer system and a printer of her own. She also neglects to mention how familiar she is with several of the major word processing packages, one of which she has used to write her CV.

As a result Jenny's CV, though well presented, tidy and attractive, is in reality not markedly different from those produced by many other graduates—people Jenny would otherwise feel to be less qualified and suited to computer work than herself.

To compound her problems, Jenny has also given her home address and telephone number, rather than her term address at university. Although in her final year and in the midst of exams, it is still four weeks before she can actually return home.

Steve highlights his training and sales experience

Before writing his CV, Steve has the sensible idea of exploring the possibilities of transferring jobs within his existing company. Realising that companies often prefer to take on people they already know, Steve seeks a meeting with a contact of his, a project manager in his company's IT department. Unfortunately, Steve discovers that no suitable vacancies currently exist. However, he does take the opportunity of discussing with the project manager some of the right and wrong ways of writing CVs and applying for computer related work.

After taking Steve through his own company's computer recruitment procedures and showing him an example of the company's computer aptitude test paper, the project manager then offers to keep Steve in mind for any future computer vacancies in the IT department.

Armed with concrete information from a real IT project manager, Steve carefully and methodically spends five evenings preparing a superb CV. Emphasising his real commercial experience and underlining some of the software and hardware platforms he has used, Steve particularly stresses his own interest and proven ability to train new computer users and his ten years' experience of selling. After it has been completed, Steve takes his handwritten CV to a professional CV writing and presentation service company. The £65 he has to pay for this service is more than justified when 20 copies of his laser printed, handsomely bound, CV are returned to him.

DISCUSSION POINTS

1. Which of your computing skills and experience do you plan to detail and emphasise in your CV?

2. In what form will you present your CV, how many copies do you think you will need to make and where do you plan to send them?

3. Given that, for computing work, a CV is the most important document you can deliver to potential employers, do you feel it is worth using and paying for the services of a professional CV writing and presentation company to prepare yours?

6
Using Computer Recruitment Agencies

Many employers in the computer industry find it both difficult and costly to fill their job vacancies. Even for junior and trainee positions, newspaper advertising regularly results in masses of applicants, many entirely unsuitable. At best, both time and effort are required to sift, select and interview potential candidates. At worst, much money and many hours are spent, only to find that no one candidate is really suitable for the job.

Conversely, for hard-to-fill posts and those for higher level positions, expensive advertising in national and local newspapers can yield relatively few suitable candidates. A full page job advert in the *Guardian*, for example, would cost an employer around £17,000 and may not result in any suitable applicants at all.

Instances like this lead many computing companies to turn to computer recruitment agencies to help them fill such posts.

UNDERSTANDING COMPUTER RECRUITMENT AGENCIES

Computer recruitment agencies act as a middle-man, a cushion between job seekers and IT employers. Basically, computer recruitment agencies charge employers (not job applicants) an agreed fee for finding suitably skilled staff for them. If no suitable staff can be found, then no fee is paid. The fee amount is normally between 15 and 40 per cent of each employee's first year's salary.

For employers, recruitment agencies provide a number of useful functions:

- They hold and maintain large databases full of information on individuals looking specifically for computer related work.

- They accept employers' instructions to search for individuals with specific computing skills or experience.

- They then search their databases for individuals with skills and experience closely matching those required by the employer.

- The speed at which these computerised searches are conducted means that agencies can often produce a list of names, addresses and contact details of likely job candidates in just a few minutes. The agency then contacts each of the people on the list to determine their level of interest in the position being offered.

- The CVs of interested individuals, already held on the agency database, are then faxed or forwarded directly to the employer, who soon has in front of him the personal details of a number of potentially suitable and interested candidates, from whom an interview short list can quickly be selected.

- The employer notifies the agency of all the candidates it would like to invite for interview. The agency then contacts each of these candidates again to arrange mutually convenient interview dates.

- If all goes well, the employer interviews his short list of candidates. The name of the successful candidate is then communicated back to the agency, which subsequently informs the candidate. After this, the agency continues to act as the middle party between the employer and the successful candidate until the candidate actually starts work, often being involved in administrative tasks like sourcing personal references as well as negotiating salary arrangements, start dates and other details with both the employer and the successful candidate.

What can computer recruitment agencies do for you?

The simple answer is that **they will do all they can to find you the computer related job you most want**.

As well as maintaining databases of potential employees, recruitment agencies also maintain databases of IT employers. The majority of these are employers who have, at some stage, indicated their interest in recruiting specifically skilled or experienced computer staff.

When you register your interest in finding computer related

work with an agency, normally by forwarding a copy of your CV and other information in a covering letter, your details are then matched against both known vacancies and interested employers on the employer database.

As interested employers are identified, the agency then, with your permission, contacts each one to discuss your suitability for the vacancy or, where no vacancy currently exists, they highlight your details and skills to the employer anyway. In this way, when vacancies do arise the employer will already be aware that you are interested in the work.

CONTACTING COMPUTER RECRUITMENT AGENCIES

Computer recruitment agencies place around 80 to 90 per cent of the advertisements commonly found in computer trade magazines such as *Computing* or *Computer Weekly*. Readers interested in the brief details given on individual vacancies are encouraged either to telephone the agency directly in order to discuss the particular position, or to fax or post a recent copy of their CV, quoting a particular reference number.

Whether you telephone in response to a particular agency advertisement or simply make a general first time enquiry, the recruitment agency will invariably ask you to send them a copy of your latest CV. In fact they may be quite reluctant to discuss any current vacancy in detail before they receive it—for commercial reasons.

Once they have received your CV, the agency will be much more forthcoming with detailed information about individual job vacancies. They will openly discuss locations, salaries, the exact nature of the position and often the name of the employer too. Also once your CV has been received, the agency will be in a far better position to advise you on the details of current vacancies you might be suitable for.

The agency will distribute your CV to individual recruitment consultants, who will assess it, and then enter it onto a computerised agency database.

If your CV shows you to have a suitable (marketable) blend of computing skills and experience, then the agency will start work on your behalf immediately. This work involves computerised skill and employer searches, followed by telephone calls and letters to employers known to have requirements for staff with your particular skills, and to employers who have, in the past, hired individuals with skills and experience similar to your own.

HELPING RECRUITMENT AGENCIES TO HELP YOU

Agencies will work very hard on your behalf if they feel it is worth it—in many cases a lot harder than you would, but they do need help occasionally. In order to continue to work effectively for you agencies need:

- to be kept up to date with changes in your personal circumstances, addresses, telephone numbers, current employment situation and particularly your current availability date

- to be kept informed of any new skills and experience you have acquired since you last contacted them

- to be told when you are no longer searching for work.

From the agency's viewpoint, receiving details of your new skills and experience effectively increases the number of positions you become potentially suitable for. Also, having your up-to-date personal details will enable them to contact you immediately when a new vacancy arises.

What happens when a suitable vacancy does arise?

When the agency identifies a vacancy which you appear to be suited for, and which the agency feels may be of interest to you, the following sequence of events will normally occur.

1. The agency contacts you, usually by telephone, to discuss the vacancy in detail and to ascertain your level of interest in the position.
2. You decide there and then whether the job sounds interesting enough to proceed further.
3. The agency, with your approval, then submits a copy of your CV, perhaps in a slightly modified form if required, to the employer.
4. The employer then considers your CV amongst any others that the same or other agencies have delivered.

5. The employer selects a short list of candidates for interview based solely on the content of the CV of each applicant.
6. The employer contacts the agency again with the names of the applicants to be invited for interview. The agency then contacts the individuals concerned to arrange interviews.

From the above, the importance of having a quality, well presented CV becomes even more apparent. It is the only document to which employers can refer when selecting candidates for interview. The quality of your CV therefore directly affects your chances of being offered interviews.

Did you know . . . ?

1. Some computer recruitment agencies will work harder than you will to find you work. In fact you may even become tired of the persistence they show on your behalf.
2. Computer recruitment agencies will always ask you to forward a copy of your CV to them. If your CV does not appeal to them they will do no work at all on your behalf. So you must make it appeal.
3. Some computer recruitment agencies will rearrange the presentation of your CV to suit the format individual employers have said they require.

Disadvantages of using computer recruitment agencies

- Agencies work best for individuals with prior computing experience.

- Agencies can sometimes be 'pushy', coercing you into applying for work you would not usually think of applying for.

- Unless you specifically instruct them otherwise, agencies may telephone you at your current place of work to discuss job details. This can be embarrassing, particularly if you work with others or in an open plan office.

- Just like everybody else, computer recruitment agencies are motivated mainly by profit. Whereas they will work extremely hard for individuals they see as having marketable skills, they may not work so diligently on behalf of those who do not.

CASE STUDIES

Dave secures a fourth interview

Dave considers computer recruitment agencies to be of marginal value to him. He knows that computer recruitment agencies work best for individuals with previous computing experience and, after all, he does have three concrete interviews arranged already. Despite this, Dave thinks it would do no harm to at least try this route. Accordingly, Dave posts copies of his CV to three local computer recruitment agencies, along with a covering letter describing the kinds of position he is looking for, emphasising his immediate availability and indicating the salary level he hopes for.

Each of the three agencies immediately responds with an acknowledgement and each gives assurances that his personal details will remain confidentially held. One agency also telephones the next day with details of a position as a junior computer operator. Although this is not quite what he wants, Dave nevertheless finds that he has been persuaded to agree to have his CV forwarded to the employer. Dave updates his own records with this information. Later that day the agency telephones back to arrange Dave's fourth interview.

Jenny decides that she needs help

After sending her CV to several potential employers in response to job advertisements she has seen, Jenny finds that, contrary to her initial thoughts, employers tend to be largely unimpressed with her degree level qualification. She looks at her CV again and realises that, in her effort to emphasise her academic achievement, she has more or less excluded all of her more practical computing skills.

She decides help is needed, and quickly. Every week spent looking for work is a week not earning any money. As a student, finances are already tight and, to Jenny, finding paid work quickly is of paramount importance.

She seeks access to the latest weekly editions of both *Computing* and *Computer Weekly*, kept for reference in the university library. From these she lists the names and contact details of 15 of the largest UK computer recruitment agencies, and begins contacting each of them to discuss some of the vacancies they had briefly advertised.

Most agencies simply ask her to forward her CV straight away, some are prepared to discuss general details about current vacancies and two are prepared to offer some advice about how to prepare a quality CV.

Jenny sets about rewriting her CV. She is extremely surprised to find that after almost two days of continuous effort, her CV, with the help of the agency's advice, looks radically different and now much better than her previous effort.

Jenny then immediately sends her new CV to all 15 agencies on her list. She believes that, by contacting so many different agencies, she will gain a far wider coverage of both geographic areas and potential employers.

Steve finds smaller agencies helpful

Since his CV has already been prepared, Steve contacts two of the smaller agencies covering his local area and is surprised to find that both invite him along for an informal lunchtime discussion about his needs. This impresses Steve, who accepts immediately. After a useful 20 minute discussion with each, Steve comes away feeling that smaller agencies might be better equipped to find him work locally than larger ones. Steve feels that this is because smaller, local agencies will have both a more detailed knowledge of more local IT employers and that they will have more time to spend on his own individual application.

In any case, Steve leaves a copy of his CV with each agency and returns to work thinking that his search for computer related work is now making real progress.

DISCUSSION POINTS

1. What, for you, would be the main advantages and disadvantages of using computer recruitment agencies to find work?

2. Larger agencies tend to deal with a wider range of IT employers than smaller, more locally based agencies. However, such employers also tend to be spread over a wider geographic area—many will be outside your job search area. In addition, larger agencies deal with larger numbers of job applicants, with correspondingly less time to spend working for individual applicants. Should you decide to use computer recruitment

agencies in your quest for IT work, would you prefer to deal with larger or smaller agencies or would you prefer a mix?

3. Should you decide to use recruitment agencies, how many will you contact and how will you ensure that each is kept fully aware of your latest skills, experience and availability for work?

7
Attending an Interview for a Computing Job

What is an interview?

At the basic level, a job interview is a meeting between yourself and one or more representatives of a potential employer. It is your opportunity to find out about them, their business and the proposed job, every bit as much as it is an opportunity for them to assess your suitability for the position on offer.

The key to successful IT interviews

The key to successful interviews for computer related vacancies lies in:

- careful preparation
- creating a good impression
- demonstrating your interest and enthusiasm for the post on offer
- demonstrating to the interview panel the benefits the company would get if they hired you rather than someone else
- successfully dealing with technical questions and computer aptitude tests.

Some facts about computing interviews

1. Many candidates will be asked to sit and pass either a computer aptitude test or a written technical test of computing knowledge, before an interview takes place.
2. Candidates can expect to be interviewed by between one and three representatives of the company. These might be, for

example, a personnel manager, the computing project manager and a technical specialist.

3. Some interviews do not involve either an aptitude test or technical questions. However, candidates should always expect and prepare for both.

PREPARING FOR A COMPUTING INTERVIEW

The key to successful interviews lies in careful preparation. By preparing carefully for your interview you will ensure that:

- you reach the interview at the correct date, time, and place
- you meet the correct people when you arrive
- you arrive armed with a good knowledge of both the company and the position on offer
- you arrive suitably presented, dressed for a 'business meeting'
- you arrive with all the items, papers and equipment that you have been requested to bring with you, or that you feel you might need
- you have the confidence to handle any written aptitude or technical test, and to answer any questions, technical or otherwise, that might be thrown at you during the course of the interview
- you arrive with a good idea of the kind of candidate the company wants to employ.

Researching the company and its prospects

Despite the fact that there may only be a few days between receiving notification and the interview itself, you will probably still have enough time to **research** the company itself, its business, its prospects and its place in the market. This will enable you to:

- impress the interview panel with your knowledge of both the company and the job itself during the interview

- assess beforehand whether the company is the type of company you would want to work for.

Sources of information for your research might include:

- the original job advertisement
- your written invitation to interview and any accompanying material
- company prospectuses, reports and advertising material
- company bulletin boards and company pages on the Internet
- company guides in your local reference library
- your local Job Centre
- the recruitment agency handling your application
- friends, relatives and existing company employees.

Practising interview techniques

If you can, arrange for somebody to give you a **mock interview**. Job Centre staff will often provide such a service, or you could ask a suitable friend, a parent or a relative—anyone who has some experience in this field.

Ask them to question you closely and to give you a realistic assessment of your performance. Though sometimes these mock interviews can be more nerve-wracking than the real thing, you will often find that the questions you have been asked during a mock interview will also be the ones asked at the real interview.

If possible, also consider asking a friend or colleague you know to be interested in computers to ask you a few technical questions about the hardware or software that you may be using in your new job. This will help you prepare and deal with the technical questions that are almost certain to be levelled at you during your interview.

Dressing for a computing interview

Almost without exception the proper dress for computing interviews is:

for men

- a dark suit with matching trousers and jacket
- a white or plain coloured collared shirt
- a sensible tie
- dark, well polished shoes and dark socks.

for women

- very smart, business-like, attire
- minimal jewellery.

In the computer industry more than most, image and presentation is everything. Some IT companies even go as far as producing a strict dress code for their employees.

What to take with you

You may have been asked by the company or recruitment agency to take various items, documents or materials with you to interview. In addition, you should also consider taking some of the following:

- evidence of your identity and the letter of invitation to interview if one exists
- pens, pencils, and an eraser—for aptitude tests
- a copy of your CV—in case the interview panel asks for it, or does not have a copy
- documentary evidence of any computer related training courses you have attended
- a sample of your past work if applicable, even if this work has been undertaken at home
- a short, written list of questions **you** intend to ask at interview.

APPROACHING A COMPUTER APTITUDE TEST

Interviews can be a little traumatic at the best of times. Interviews for many IT positions also carry an additional sting in the tail in the form of a computer aptitude test of some kind. Such tests often precede interviews, and many employers insist that they be successfully completed prior to an interview taking place.

What is a computer aptitude test?

There are various forms of computer aptitude test in common use by IT employers. The most common consists of a document, booklet or question sheet containing questions which involve applying some form of logic to solve. Some examples are shown later in this chapter.

Candidates are normally asked to write their answers on the test paper itself and must occasionally also hand in accompanying sheets of paper provided for workings, mathematical calculations and other notes.

Some companies eschew aptitude or 'logic' tests in favour of setting more technically oriented tests. Such technically biased tests are designed to assess the candidate's depth of computing knowledge and, more specifically, their knowledge of individual software packages or hardware platforms.

Aptitude, technical and other forms of written test are becoming increasingly common in the computer industry. This is particularly true for vacancies for:

- computer programmers
- hardware engineers
- software engineers
- systems analysts.

Some facts about computer aptitude tests

1. A fixed amount of time is usually allotted for the test, normally 30 minutes, 45 minutes or one hour.
2. More questions are set than it is normally possible to answer. Candidates are not expected to be able to complete all questions.
3. Accuracy in the questions that are answered is more important than the number of questions answered.
4. There is normally a logical method of solving each problem set. Once this method has been found, then actually answering the

question will only involve simple arithmetic, or process of elimination. It is the candidate's ability to derive the correct method of solving the problem that is of most importance.

Preparing for an aptitude test

For written tests of a technical nature:

- Revise and study your software, hardware and other technical books and manuals for several days prior to the interview. If possible, ask friends or colleagues to test your technical knowledge. Revise your documentation for those questions you cannot answer satisfactorily.

For aptitude, logic and psychometric type tests:

- Buy one of the many available books of logic tests and practise doing some questions. Such books can be bought quite cheaply from all major book shops. Some newsagents also stock magazines with similar kinds of tests. Although it is unlikely that any of the questions will be the same as those you encounter in an employer's aptitude test, they will nevertheless give you some important clues about how to approach these types of questions. Consider the following questions, typical of their kind. The answers are given in Appendix A. (The questions should be considered to have been taken from the easier sections of an IT employer's aptitude test.)

Section one—short questions

(Typically 30–50 questions in about 15 minutes.)

1. What is the next number in the sequence: 1, 3, 5, 7, 11, 13, 17 . . . ?
2. What is the next letter in the sequence: W T F S S M . . . ?
3. What is the next word in the sequence: bit byte kilobyte . . . ?
4. Complete the following: Black is to white as night is to . . .

These are typical of the shorter type of questions aptitude tests contain. Shorter questions tend to be grouped in lots of 30–50 per section. Frequently there is not enough time to complete all questions, though this is not the main aim. Employers are more concerned with the accuracy achieved in the answers.

Section two—longer questions

(Typically 10–15 questions in about 30 minutes.)

Longer questions, often in groups of ten, also regularly appear in computer aptitude tests. Consider the following:

5. A man got into a lift on the bottom floor of a 100 storey building. As the lift was rising the man exclaimed, 'I've missed my floor. The floor I wanted to get off on was 15 more than the square root of the floor I am now on.' Since the man was just less than half way up the building what floor was he currently on and what floor did he really want to get off at?

CREATING A GOOD IMPRESSION AT A COMPUTER INTERVIEW

Providing you pass any set aptitude test, you will shortly be led into the interview room to meet a panel of normally up to three company representatives.

Shaking hands

Ensure that you offer your hand to be shaken by each member of the panel, repeat their names as you shake their hands if you can. Wait until being invited to take your nominated seat in the room before sitting down. Relax. Make yourself comfortable in the chair and smile. This is the moment you have prepared for. Wait until a member of the interview panel speaks to you.

Like interviews conducted the world over, IT interviews often begin with the interviewer asking how far you have travelled, how you got there, or some other question designed to start the conversation and put you at your ease.

This is your first opportunity to speak. Do so clearly, confidently and honestly. If the question is about the method of travel to interview state that you had no problems getting there. Say this was because you had conducted a dry run the day before; immediate evidence of the fact that you have prepared well for the interview and that you are organised and efficient.

IT interviews will often begin in earnest with the chairperson of the panel describing the company, the job on offer and generally supplying background information such as the nature of the computers they manufacture, the software they supply or the IT services they provide. Having prepared and researched well, most of this information will already be familiar to you.

However, do not interrupt, let the chairperson speak. When this opening preamble is finished, reply with an interesting fact if possible. Call on your research findings to say something about the company or its products which members of the panel may not know. This, in addition to your earlier comment, will convince the panel that your preparation has been better than that of most of the other interview candidates.

Learning by example

As an example of how to impress at a computer interview let us now examine a relatively short but revealing extract from a mythical, but nevertheless realistic, IT interview for a trainee computer programmer. Notice how the content of the candidate's responses highlights his past achievements and emphasises his strengths, skills and experience. Notice how this leads the panel to believing that the candidate, after only a couple of minutes of the interview have elapsed, is probably the successful candidate.

Chairperson: Come in, Mr Smith, please sit down and make yourself comfortable. My name is Mr Harris. I am Software Solution's personnel manager. On my right is Mrs Davies, project leader for the Orion software project, and to my left is Mr Giggs, a senior programmer also on the Orion project. I see that you live in Aylesbury—have you travelled far?

Candidate: Good morning, Mr Harris. Well, Aylesbury is around 25 miles from here. I came up in the car yesterday to find out where Software Solutions was, and I am glad to say that my journey today was trouble free and only took about 40 minutes.

Later.

Chairperson: Well, Mr Smith, I have explained what Software Solutions is all about, the rapid growth we have experienced over the past three years and the plentiful opportunities that exist for career minded people within the company. Can you now tell the panel a little bit about yourself, your background and what qualities you will bring to Software Solutions should you be offered the post?

Candidate: Yes, I can. Thank you for that. I remember reading that Software Solutions became the 53rd largest software company in the UK earlier this year and that you were the first software company south of Birmingham to introduce a dedicated bulletin board service for your customers.

I am 17 years old and have just left Aylesbury Sixth Form College with two 'A' levels, including an 'A' grade in computing. I captained the school's rugby team for three years and also ran the 400 metre hurdles event at county level. I am also interested in collecting historical sporting facts and figures. To this end, and about 18 months ago, I bought a small personal computer with the aim of writing a small but fully functional database program to store and retrieve these facts. At first, I naively thought I could write the software in around two to three weeks using Microsoft VISUAL BASIC version 4.0 running in a Windows 95 environment. I was soon proved wrong. It ended up taking me three times as long and I spent most nights for about nine weeks writing and perfecting the program. It works well and I have enjoyed using it.

Since then, I have come to realise that it must be quite difficult to estimate accurately how long software takes to write. A rule of thumb I use nowadays for my own projects is to arrive at an approximate estimate and then double it. For some reason this has always ended up being far more accurate.

Since writing my database, I have written a number of smaller VISUAL BASIC programs—again at home, and I have recently started to learn how to use and program version 7.0 of a database called 'Paradox' by Borland.

For my 'A' level computing project, I developed a small computer game using the 'C' programming language—Microsoft VISUAL 'C/C++' Version 2.0.

Chairperson: That's interesting, we make extensive use of 'C' here at Software Solutions. What made you choose 'C' for your school project when you were already familiar with VISUAL BASIC at home?

Candidate: Yes, I understand that Software Solutions uses 'C' on the Orion project. That is why I was particularly keen to apply for this vacancy. I chose 'C' for my game because I had been advised that 'C', though more complex and generally more difficult to write software with than VISUAL BASIC, would produce faster, smaller programs. I needed speed of processing for my game because the graphics and rapid movement of objects such as missiles and bombs tended to be very processor intensive. I also felt that because I knew VISUAL BASIC already, using 'C' for the first time would be much more of a challenge. It was. It was worth it though. I now know 'C' pretty well, though I admit I still have a lot to learn. Actually, I took the liberty of bringing along some of the program listings for my game, just in case you might want to see them.

Chairperson: Did you? Goodness. Yes we would be pleased to see them.

SPEAKING CONFIDENTLY, HANDLING TECHNICAL QUESTIONS

The above extract, though mythical, would nevertheless have led most interview panels to sit up and take notice of this apparently bright, confident and enthusiastic young man who had obviously prepared well for the interview.

The applicant has shown strong evidence of his previous computing experience, his technical ability with named software products, and a realistic appreciation of some of the problems involved with writing software. He has shown he is not afraid to learn new skills—in fact he welcomes the challenge and, to top it all, has even taken the initiative to bring in samples of his work just in case they might be needed.

The interview panel would probably not notice or even care that Mr Smith had failed his third 'A' level completely and only just passed his second 'A' level with an 'E' grade.

The candidate has also successfully emphasised his strengths as they relate to the particular vacancy applied for—the candidate mentioned his 'C' experience, for example.

From his experiences with VISUAL BASIC and particularly with 'C', the panel are left in no doubt as to the candidate's technical ability. In fact they were probably reassured to hear the candidate honestly admit that there were some things about the 'C' language he still had to learn—remember the position on offer is one of 'trainee computer programmer'.

On the whole the candidate has remained upbeat, confident and interesting throughout. He has even surprised the interview panel by offering real examples of his work in the form of paper program listings—without appearing to be bigheaded in any way.

At no time has he argued or disagreed with the chairperson. He has remained polite throughout and has always allowed the chairperson to finish his question before giving a response.

He has also managed in relatively few words, and over the span of just a few minutes, to persuade the interview panel that he has thoroughly researched the company, its products and the software it uses, and by implication has shown he has a reasonable idea of the type of position on offer.

From the evidence so far, there would seem little point in the panel asking the candidate technical programming questions. He has already given the impression that he would be more than capable of answering most of them.

However, for illustrative purposes let us examine what might happen if technical questions were asked and how the candidate might answer them.

Mr Giggs: As Mr Harris explained, I am a senior programmer on the Orion project. I am going to ask you a few technical questions. These questions are not intended to embarrass or confuse. They are simply intended to find the limits of your technical knowledge rather than to explore what you do not know. I hope you do not mind?

Candidate: Not at all.

Mr Giggs: What are the main problems you have found using 'C' as opposed to using VISUAL BASIC to write your software?

Candidate: Several problems spring to mind immediately. 'C' is a much more complex and difficult language to program with than VISUAL BASIC—it's also a lot more powerful. Also with 'C' it is much more likely that a programming mistake will go unnoticed for a while. These programming mistakes or 'bugs' often cause system crashes when they finally reveal themselves. Bugs in 'C' programs can often be difficult to track down and put right—using a quality 'C' debugging program to find such bugs is almost a necessity for larger programs. Because of these problems, not so prevalent with VISUAL BASIC, 'C' programs almost invariably take a lot longer to write, test and debug. In return for this, however, 'C' programs tend to be much smaller, more memory efficient and run much more quickly—up to 100 times more quickly, I have read.

Mr Giggs: You mention program debuggers. How extensively have you used them?

Candidate: At first I used to try to hunt down program bugs simply by looking through the program listing. However, I quickly found the 'C' debugger to be of immense help. I use it all the time now. All in all I have about four months' experience of using the Microsoft debugger.

Mr Giggs: Have you ever used the integral assembler incorporated in some 'C' compilers? We use this facility a lot here at Orion.

Candidate: No, I haven't. But I do know that they allow programmers to gain lower level access to the registers within the computer micro processor. I also know that my own 'C' compiler has such a facility. I would be interested to learn how to use the assembler in this way. I know that already fast running 'C' programs can be speeded up even more using this method.

The candidate has answered all questions, including the last one, perfectly well. Indeed for each question, the candidate has carefully offered a lot more information than was actually asked for.

He has also been honest. He has admitted to not having used the integral assembler facility within his 'C' compiler, even though he has plainly demonstrated an awareness of its existence and its purpose. From a technical viewpoint the only qualms a panel might have at this stage would be those of worrying whether the 'trainee' position on offer was too junior for this obviously competent candidate.

Let us summarise what we have learned about how candidates should attend and handle IT interviews. Model candidates attending IT interviews are:

- **well prepared**—having researched both the company and as much as possible about the position on offer
- **enthusiastic**—willing to go 'the extra mile' to secure the vacancy on offer
- **polite**—not at all controversial
- **confident**—but not over confident, arrogant or bigheaded
- **positive**—accentuating their strengths, selling their skills, achievements and experience and seldom using words like 'not', 'never', 'no', 'do not', 'cannot' except where these are appropriate
- **honest**—admitting lack of knowledge where this is the case

- **articulate**—ready to talk about technical issues and to mention individual products, manufacturers, model names, software version numbers and other computer terminology

- **interested** in computers and willing to demonstrate this interest by describing home, school or spare time activities and computer projects.

Three non technical questions commonly asked at computing interviews

1. What do you know about the position on offer?
2. How would you feel about working as a member of a small team?
3. When would you be available for work should you be offered the position this week?

Top tips for candidates attending computer interviews

1. Arrive punctually, well dressed and fully prepared for the interview.
2. Take some examples of your own work with you even if they have not been specifically requested. You may get the opportunity to impress the interview panel with them.
3. Always be prepared to admit that there are some areas of your subject of which you have limited or no technical knowledge.
4. Remain confident and positive throughout the interview.
5. Do not argue, directly disagree or otherwise antagonise the interview panel. However, state your views firmly, expressing logical reasons for them and do not be swayed from them, however provoked. Also ensure that you allow the interviewer to finish what he is saying before giving your response.
6. Concentrate on keeping eye contact with the person with whom you are communicating at all times.
7. Stress your skills, strengths and experience. 'Go the extra mile' to show how you above all others are the right candidate for the job.
8. Always indicate that you are prepared to talk about technical issues.
9. Never criticise your current employer if you have one.
10. Smile, remain polite, and do not get flustered. Some panels purposely try to provoke candidates to assess their reaction. Try to stay calm at all times.

11. Always answer the question asked. Do not give 'politicians' answers, though by all means do give extra, supporting information if this is relevant.
12. Critically analyse your performance after the interview is over. Learn any lessons and resolve to improve your performance in what you perceive as your weak areas for next time.

ASKING QUESTIONS OF YOUR OWN

Towards the end of the interview you will normally be given the opportunity to ask some questions of your own. Produce your prepared list and do not be frightened to read from it. Ideally you should ask between one and three questions. If you do not have any questions to ask you may risk the panel thinking that you lack interest in the position. Conversely, asking more than three might become a little boring and time consuming.

Your questions should avoid going over ground that has previously been covered and should be designed to:

- clear up any residual facts you might wish to know

- further demonstrate your interest in the position on offer.

Some questions you might ask at an IT interview

1. What are the company's future plans to remain competitive in the computer market?
2. What opportunities are there for promotion within the IT section of this company?
3. Does the company intend to move offices to another location or will it remain here for the foreseeable future?

Some questions to avoid asking at computer interviews

1. Are you negotiable on the level of salary and benefits package you offer?
2. Why is your staff turnover higher than the average for the computer industry? (This question is best answered by talking to people outside the context of a formal job interview.)
3. Should I be offered the position, would you be prepared to wait six weeks until I become available for work?

Question time

I have heard that some computing companies use pre-printed forms for assessing candidates' performances at interview. Is this true and if so can you give an example of one?
Yes, it is true. There is no one standard layout for forms of this kind but Figure 13 is typical of its kind.

Is there anything I can do after I have left the interview room to increase my chances of being offered the job?
Yes. Firstly, leave the site immediately. If a computer recruitment agency arranged the interview on your behalf, telephone them as soon as possible to discuss how the interview went. This will ensure that the agency is kept fully informed on your progress. It will also help the agency negotiate on your behalf to secure you the job on the best terms possible if it is offered. If you found the interview yourself, do nothing for a few days. If, after say three or four days you have heard nothing, consider telephoning the company to speak to a member of the interview panel. Explain how much you want the position and ask if there is anything else you could do that would finally convince the company to offer the position to you. This may not achieve anything, but it is unlikely to count against you when the final decision is made.

COMPLETING THE INTERVIEW IN STYLE

The end of the interview should be conducted with the minimum of fuss. By all means ask one or two questions or briefly reiterate your enthusiasm and availability for the post. Then rise from your seat, shake hands with each member of the panel, remembering to repeat their names as you do so. Say your goodbyes, then leave the building promptly.

CASE STUDIES

Dave distinguishes himself from all other candidates

Dave has a particularly pleasant problem to solve. With four interviews over the course of a week, he has the task of researching four different companies, establishing the job descriptions of each of the four positions on offer, and planning all of his travel arrangements. However, Dave still manages to prepare thoroughly.

Computer Hardware & Software Ltd

Interview Assessment Form

A = Excellent, B = Good, C = Satisfactory,
D = Less than satisfactory, E = Poor

Candidate's name : ________________
Position applied for : ________________

Aptitude test result : ________%

	Grading
Punctuality	______
General appearance	______
Dress	______
Manner and attitude	______
Facility with spoken word	______
Knowledge of company	______
Knowledge of position on offer	______
Qualifications	______
Technical skills	______
Initiative	______
Previous experience	______
Stability of previous employment	______
Availability	______
Overall assessment	______

Notes

Fig. 13. A sample form used to assess performance at interview.

On the day of the first interview—for a position as trainee programmer—Dave leaves home early to ensure he reaches the company's offices punctually. He announces himself at reception and is soon led into the interview room. No aptitude test has been set.

Slightly nervous in front of the two interviewers, Dave initially feels a little overawed by his surroundings, but is soon at his ease when the conversation turns to Dave's favourite subject—computers. He remembers that it is an equally difficult task for the interviewers to find a suitable candidate as it is for him to persuade them that he is the right candidate for the job. This reassures him as he begins to impress the panel with technical details of the computer he owns and some of the software he has written at home and at school.

At an appropriate moment, Dave produces some of his computer listings and the floppy disk he has brought along which contains a copy of a program he has written. The panel are impressed and more so when Dave suggests that a PC in the corner be turned on so that he can give them a proper demonstration of his work. The panel agree and are subsequently treated to an interesting ten minute visual display of Dave's programming talents.

At the end of the interview, Dave asks just two questions of his own. Then, before leaving, he shakes hands with each panel member, repeating their names as he does so.

After Dave has gone, the two panel members look at one another. This is the first interview either has ever undertaken in which the candidate went to the trouble to bring in program listings and a computer disk in order to physically demonstrate his work. They both agree that Dave's initiative, preparedness and enthusiasm outweigh all other factors. In fact they have not even discussed academic achievement or other technical issues at all.

Dave's immediate availability for work is the icing on the cake for the interview panel. The vacancy needs filling quickly and here is a candidate with demonstrable skills, enthusiasm, interest and who is available to start work straight away. Both interviewers agree that Dave has more than distinguished himself from the three other candidates they have seen, despite their superior academic qualifications. Accordingly they decide that Dave should be made a firm offer of the job.

Jenny finally secures two interviews

Jenny is beginning to recover from her faltering start. Her revamped CV is now beginning to impress. Two computer recruitment agencies out of the 15 she has contacted have managed to secure interviews on her behalf—the first as a software engineer and the second for a customer support position. Though both are in locations Jenny has not thought of working in she is nevertheless eager to attend and do well at each. To this effect she carefully prepares, researching the two companies, contacting the two agencies for a more detailed picture of the positions on offer and practising her interview technique in mock interviews conducted by two of her fellow students.

She arrives on time at the first interview and is immediately invited to sit a computer aptitude test. Despite her degree standard education and proven proficiency in using and programming computers, Jenny finds the test a lot more difficult than she thought it would be. Thirty minutes later, Jenny is politely told she has failed the test and that no interview will therefore take place.

Shattered by this experience, Jenny vows never again to be caught out like this. She immediately purchases a book of logic tests similar to the ones she has just failed and begins practising.

Ironically, there is no written aptitude test at Jenny's second interview. Jenny finds that the interview panel of three are more interested in finding out what Jenny thinks a customer support position is, how well she can communicate and what qualities she feels she would bring to the job.

Thanks to her mock interviews, Jenny is well prepared to answer these questions. Gaining confidence all the time, Jenny soon finds the panel asking when she could start work. Jenny explains that she would first need a little time to find suitable accommodation in the area, but that she would probably start within two weeks of any firm, written offer being made.

Steve prepares well for his only interview

Steve manages to secure an interview for a position in the sales department of a local company manufacturing computer components. Preparing well for this, his only immediate chance of finding work within the computer industry, Steve feels that his best chance of success will be to try to discover as much about the company, computer sales, and the company's customers as possible. Already familiar with sales environments, Steve knows that the computer sales industry will be entirely customer focused. His preparation therefore concentrates on finding out how the company currently attracts and keeps customers and how these methods might be improved.

Steve arrives punctually at the interview. He is surprised to find only one person interviewing him, but immediately feels comfortable talking about computer sales. His previous experience of selling and administering insurance policies, coupled with his research findings, mean that Steve is confidently able to sell himself to the interviewer.

Steve leaves the interview feeling that he has given a good account of himself and that his studious preparation has definitely paid off.

Nevertheless, Steve shortly begins to feel a little uncertain about what the job itself might actually entail on a day to day basis. In particular, he wishes he had asked during the interview about such things as how much travel would be involved and what opportunities there were for promotion. With hindsight he wishes he had spent some of his preparation building a list of questions he could ask.

DISCUSSION POINTS

1. What steps will you take to ensure that you reach the interview room on time, relaxed and fully prepared?

2. Computer aptitude tests seem to present just as many difficulties to graduates and existing computer professionals as they do to complete novices. In addition, they are fast becoming a standard method by which employers in the computer industry select candidates for interview. In view of this, how will you ensure that you are prepared for any aptitude test you might be asked to sit?

3. How do you intend to emphasise your strengths, skills and qualities to interview panels without appearing to be over confident or big headed?

8
Responding to a Job Offer

Assuming all has gone well and you are selected as the successful candidate, the next thing you will experience is the rather pleasant feeling of being made an offer of a job!

What is a job offer?

A job offer is a conditional or unconditional **offer of employment** made by an employer to a successful job applicant. Such offers can be oral or written.

Considering job offers

Although you may first become aware of a job offer by telephone, it should not be considered concrete until a written offer has been received. A written offer represents documented evidence that an employer wishes to enter into a contract of employment with you. You should always wait until a written offer has been received before either studying it in detail or responding to it.

Examining conditional and unconditional offers

Offers of employment will be either **conditional** or **unconditional**. If conditional, then the conditions will be specified in full. These conditions must be met by the candidate and, in some cases, by the company, before the offer can be considered firm.

The following are examples of some of the more typical conditions specified within written job offers of the kind made by IT employers:

- 'subject to a satisfactory medical, eye test or declaration of health'
- 'subject to the candidate passing a government security check'

—this is particularly common in offers made by IT companies working on sensitive defence or other government related projects where the candidate is required to be given access to restricted, confidential or secret information

- 'subject to satisfactory references being received'
- 'subject to the employer winning a specific new piece of business or being awarded a new contract . . .'

The first three types of condition are standard and should present no real concerns or problems to most candidates. The fourth is a little more worrying. It means that the employer is making the offer conditional on it winning new business. As such, the vacancy does not yet really exist.

A unconditional offer is made when an employer is happy that a candidate already satisfies all of its employment conditions.

STUDYING A JOB OFFER

Written offers of employment can vary widely depending on the type of position on offer. Figure 14 shows a sample offer letter, typical of its kind, and addressed to the successful candidate interviewed for a post as a hardware maintenance and repair technician.

All the important details concerning the job offer have been included in the letter shown in Figure 14. They are as follows:

- location of work
- nature of work or job title
- starting salary and details of other benefits offered
- annual holiday entitlement
- a preliminary start date
- details of working hours

Computer Hardware Maintenance Ltd
12 Employer Road, London SW1 5FX
Tel: (0171) 345 345

Mr David Noble,
68 Hilltop Drive,
Lower Westbury,
London SW1 1DD.

24 September 199X

Dear David,

Further to your recent interview, I am delighted to offer you the position of Computer Repair and Maintenance Technician (Grade 5). You are invited to start work on 15 October 199X.

The remuneration package we are offering includes:

(a) A starting salary of £13,500 per annum. This will be increased to £13,800 in January 199X and reviewed every six months thereafter.
(b) A contributory Pension Scheme (details enclosed).
(c) Membership of the company's comprehensive Private Health Care and Medical Insurance Plans.
(d) 20 days paid holiday annually, rising to 22 days after three years' service.
(e) Use of a company car for both business and private mileage.

You will initially be based at our depot in Employer Road, London, but as you are aware, the work may require you to be located at client sites from time to time and this could involve you having to work away from your home and family for short periods. If you do, then all of your out-of-pocket expenses will be reimbursed in full.

The company works a standard 37.5 hour week. Normal working hours are 9.00am–5.00pm Monday to Friday. Any agreed overtime will be paid on a pro rata basis.

We all very much look forward to seeing you on the 15th, but please note that this offer is conditional upon receipt of both satisfactory references and a signed Declaration of Health (enclosed).

I would be grateful if you would confirm your acceptance and start date in writing, within ten working days. Please also sign and return the Declaration of Health.

In the meantime if you have any problems meeting this time scale, or any queries regarding this offer, please do not hesitate to contact me.

Yours sincerely,

James Lewis
Personnel Manager

Fig. 14. A written job offer.

- any conditions which relate to the offer
- sundry details.

Examining job location

Apart from salary and perhaps the nature of the job on offer, its location is perhaps the factor which will most influence your decision to accept or decline it.

When assessing the offer you should examine both the personal and financial consequences of possibly having to:

- commute on a daily basis to and from the place of work
- relocate or find suitable accommodation near to the place of work
- work at locations other than the main location for any length of time
- travel to customer sites and other locations during the working day. This is particularly relevant to jobs in computer sales, computer training, customer support and hardware maintenance.

Examining the type of position on offer

Check that the position on offer is the same position you originally applied for. Check also to ensure that no significant changes or additions have been made to the original job description.

Always ask yourself whether the position on offer will really be one that you will enjoy. Although finding a job in computers may be your main aim, there are myriad different job types within the IT industry as a whole. Ensure that this particular position is exactly the one you want.

Weighing up starting salary and benefits packages

Ensure that the salary offered is at least sufficient to provide you with a reasonable standard of living. It should also be broadly in line with job market rates.

As well as salary, IT companies, along with many others, often provide a package of benefits. This package might typically include such things as:

- membership of a company pension scheme
- private health or medical insurance
- overtime at enhanced rates
- a sick pay scheme
- company shares and other bonus schemes
- mortgages or loans at preferential rates
- use of a company car
- annual paid holiday entitlement
- preferential staff prices for the company's products.

Some of the financial implications of such benefits can often more than outweigh a slightly lower than average salary.

Paid holidays are important too. Most reputable IT companies will offer around 20–25 days paid holiday each year—in addition to standard bank holidays. Check to make sure that your written offer contains such details, and that they are acceptable.

Considering start dates, working hours and overtime payments

Most IT companies specify a 35–40 hour working week, and a standard 9.00 a.m.–5.00 p.m. working day or close to this. For some types of computing jobs, computer operators for example, some night time or shift work may be required.

Many companies in the computer industry do not offer to pay for overtime working. You will need to be clear about the prospect of overtime working and the financial rewards, if any, that accompany it.

Reading the small print

Written job offers are seldom prepared to deceive the candidate into blindly accepting the job. Far from it.

Sundry and miscellaneous details are often included to help both the candidate and the company reach agreement as soon as possible.

Typically a written offer will contain important details such as:

- a date by which the company has asked the candidate to respond to its offer
- where and to whom you should report on your first day
- what to bring with you when you start work.

NEGOTIATING TERMS AND CONDITIONS

Apart from the most junior computing positions, where salary, benefits and conditions are largely inflexible, most offers of employment for positions within the computer industry are negotiable—within limits.

Exactly what is negotiable?

In theory everything about the offer is negotiable. In practice, however, the following list specifies what is normally negotiable for a computer related job.

Normally negotiable	*Normally not negotiable*
Starting salary	Hours of work
Start date	Holiday entitlement
Provision of some benefits such as a company car	Nature of the work
	Location of work
	Established commission or company bonus schemes
	Conditions that apply to the offer of work
	Frequency and dates of salary payments
	Sick pay schemes
	Notice periods

Successful negotiation depends on both parties feeling that a fair deal has been struck.

Your negotiating position will be determined amongst other things by:

- the existence or otherwise of alternative employment offers
- your own financial situation and current level of income
- the location of the work offered
- your own negotiating skills or those of your recruitment agency who will, incidentally, often be prepared to negotiate on your behalf.

Conversely, the employer's willingness to negotiate the terms of its offer will be affected largely by:

- the urgency with which it needs to fill the post
- the number of other candidates considered suitable for the position
- the extent of the current candidate's suitability for the position
- the candidate's attitude towards negotiating.

ACCEPTING THE OFFER

Once you have studied and possibly negotiated the offer, the time has come for you to decide once and for all whether the job is really for you.

If you decide to accept the offer, your acceptance should be sent, in writing, to the writer of the offer letter, within the deadline originally specified. Remember to include in your acceptance letter a reference to the original offer letter and a confirmation that you intend to start work on the proposed start date. Once this has been completed, the next stage is to prepare for work.

Declining job offers

You should think very seriously about declining job offers. If you are fortunate enough to be sitting on more than one offer, then clearly one will have to be declined.

Inevitably, some employers expect, and plan for, a certain percentage of candidates to decline job offers, but in every case they wish to be made aware of this as soon as possible.

At the end of the day, it is you, your family and your career that are ultimately affected by your decision to accept or decline work. The final decision is yours.

Did you know . . . ?

1. Many employers expect to have to negotiate salaries and benefits with successful job applicants.
2. Recruitment agencies will often negotiate higher salaries and better terms with employers than you would.
3. By far the quickest and most effective method of winning promotion within the computer industry is to move to another company. Spend two or three years there—working hard, gaining new skills and experience, and then move on again.

PREPARING FOR A JOB IN COMPUTERS

Once your letter of acceptance has been dispatched, you can then look forward to starting work on the agreed date.

Successful candidates approaching the start date for their new computing job will be gratified to know that there is scope for preparation which will considerably ease first day nerves.

Equipping yourself for IT work

You can start by gathering together all of the necessary equipment which might be needed at your new place of work. For jobs in the computer industry these might include such items as:

- pens, pencils, rulers, erasers, calculators
- diary, set square, personal organiser
- technical manuals and computer books
- a notebook

- a small toolkit (for hardware related positions)
- notes you have made in preparation for work
- tax forms like the P45 and National Insurance number card
- your bank account details for salary payment
- any items you have specifically been asked to bring along.

A smart brief case will enhance your professional image and will also provide a mechanism for carrying much of the above.

Employees transferring between jobs may need to take tax forms such as their P45. For everyone else, employers will at least need a note of your National Insurance number.

Reading

The normally short time between accepting and actually taking up an IT job can profitably be spent reading some of the more specialised books or computer manuals you have access to.

Just as you prepare for a technical interview by reading, studying and revising your technical literature, so you can prepare for starting work in the same way. You will already know what software, hardware or services your new employer uses or supplies. Another visit to the library or local bookshop to stock up on relevant publications will always be worthwhile. Indeed, any preparation in this area will undoubtedly add to your confidence and greatly ease your transition into the new job.

Practising your computer skills

If you have access to a computer at home or elsewhere, then consider using it to practise your technical skills or even to learn new ones. In the computer industry, more than most, your technical skills, in either hardware or software related positions, are the key to your success—at least earlier on in your computing career. As the years pass and you naturally progress up the company hierarchy, technical skills will normally be superseded by new types of skills such as how to manage staff and control computer projects.

Early on though, technical skills are everything. The more you are able to practise before you actually start work the better prepared and more confident you will feel.

Forming a career plan

In the IT industry promotion is almost solely based on merit. This means that the right individuals can often find themselves in senior positions with IT related companies very early on in their career.

The following career plan is typical for a talented programmer leaving school at 16 or 18. Several changes of company may be required to progress more quickly.

Age 16–18	Trainee programmer
Age 20	Computer programmer
Age 25	Senior programmer
Age 30	Senior software/hardware engineer, or team leader, computer consultant
Age 35	Project leader
Age 40	Software development manager, senior manager, head of IT, senior or principal consultant
Age 45	Board level manager.

Relaxing, enjoyment and quality of life

However you decide to prepare for your first day in your new computing job, do not forget to relax and take things easy for a while too. In the fast moving, ever changing world of IT, stress, pressure of work and a sedentary lifestyle can often lead to health and other problems later on in life. So whatever you do, do not forget to relax occasionally and enjoy the fruits of your labours.

CASE STUDIES

Dave quickly accepts his first job offer

Dave's outstanding performance at interview leads to a written offer of employment as a trainee programmer at a salary of £8,800 per year for a 40 hour working week. Dave could not have wished for more. Being young and eager to start work and to begin earning money as soon as possible, Dave quickly accepts what is, in reality, an offer at slightly less than average terms.

Dave has just four days to spend reading, practising and relaxing before his first big day at work. At 16, Dave is just pleased to have been successful in securing a full time job in computing. He justifiably feels that planning a longer term career strategy could be left for a while.

Looking back, Dave feels that the keys to his success lay in careful interview preparation and in his ability to convey his practical computing knowledge and innate interest in computers to the interview panel.

Jenny learns of her success through the recruitment agency

Jenny learns of her success at interview via the computer recruitment agency that submitted her application. Jenny is elated at first. Finances are tight and her new job will finally give her the chance to do something about her large bank overdraft. However, her joy is tempered by realism. Jenny quickly begins thinking of the real world implications of taking the job—the cost of travel, relocation and the fact that this particular job is perhaps not the one she really wanted.

She openly discusses this with her recruitment agency. The agency helpfully mentions that the employer might be willing to bear some of the cost of relocating, and that they are prepared to negotiate with the employer on Jenny's behalf, if required.

Later that day the agency telephones to say that the company will bear the first £250 of Jenny's relocation expenses and, to Jenny's surprise, have offered a further £750 per year on top of the £14,500 salary already offered. Both Jenny's agency and her new employer have obviously gone to some lengths on her behalf.

As a result, she accepts the offer of employment and spends the time up until she starts work finding and setting up home in new rented accommodation close to her new employers' main offices.

On reflection, Jenny feels that the main lessons she learned whilst looking for IT work are that producing a top quality CV is vital, and that candidates should always be adequately prepared to meet computer aptitude tests.

Steve receives an appealing job offer

Steve receives an offer of a job in computer component sales. The offer specifies a starting salary of £16,500 per year and free use of a company car. For Steve this represents a salary increase of £1,500 per year. On top of this Steve has never had a company car before.

His own car is beginning to age and become costly to run. This offer appears to be very appealing indeed at first sight.

However, Steve is right to have reservations. He has yet to clarify such details as what the job actually involves on a day to day basis, and exactly how much travel it will entail.

Steve rightly feels that, before making a final decision, he ought to telephone the company to clarify these details. After all, he already has a reasonably good, stable job with his current employer and is not going to give it up for a job he knows relatively little about.

Steve quickly discovers that having the company car will mean substantial amounts of daily travel to and from customer sites and that, although the job is principally a 9.00 a.m. to 5.00 p.m. job, in reality, lots of evening and weekend work will be required. Future salary increases are also linked to his sales performance.

In the light of this new information, Steve realises that, for him, the offer is not as appealing as he first thought. After discussions with his wife, Steve decides to decline the offer. On balance, he feels he would be better off remaining in his current job whilst continuing his search for more suitable, more appealing work.

Steve's patience and level headed attitude soon pay off. Within weeks he is interviewed for, and subsequently offered, a job in the training division of his own company's IT department. Steve is offered an increased salary, more responsibility, a wider variety of work, and the opportunity to use computers on a day to day basis. He gladly accepts.

DISCUSSION POINTS

1. What salary expectations do you have from your first job in computers?

2. What factors would most influence you when considering an offer of a job in the computer industry?

3. What steps will you take to ensure that you arrive at work on your first day fully prepared for a new job in computers?

9
Finding Computer Jobs Abroad

COMPUTING OVERSEAS

Computer job opportunities for UK nationals overseas have never been greater.

Up to now, most computing jobs overseas have tended to be in the form of fixed length assignments typically of up to two years in duration. This will continue to be the case in many non EU countries. However, the Single European Market, which came into being in 1993, means that more and more people are beginning to apply for and take up permanent IT jobs within the European Union.

Why work in computers abroad?

Computer professionals eager to take up work overseas cite several reasons for wanting to do so:

- to travel, to experience new cultures and to learn a new language
- for better rates of pay
- for more variety of work
- because working in computers abroad for a while can sometimes make individuals more in demand when they return back home.

To balance the benefits of working in computers abroad, some people state that:

- having to learn a new language

- the pressure of living and working in a foreign environment where they may be classed a minority group
- higher rates of taxation
- less attractive working conditions

are reasons why they would think carefully about living and working in IT abroad.

Computing in an EU country

EU countries offer the experienced computer professional a wealth of opportunities. The key word here is **experienced**. Though work and travel regulations, in theory, permit EU employees to freely take up work and to reside in any of the EU member countries, inexperienced computer staff have little chance of finding their first job in computers outside their own country.

For the seasoned computer professional, however, the picture is vastly different. With English spoken widely in EU member states, particularly within IT companies, many of the barriers that inhibit inexperienced individuals abroad simply do not exist for experienced staff.

IT employers in the EU are far more concerned about recruiting the right computing skills than they are about the nationality of the person who has the skills. Having the right skills to work in the EU is, just as in the UK, the key to finding IT related work.

For UK nationals, adapting to a job in Europe also appears to present no real problems. Less than ten per cent return home before they anticipated doing so. Most quickly settle down to working in their new environment.

Computing in a non EU country

Computing jobs in non EU countries are generally more difficult to secure than those inside the EU. Inexperienced individuals in particular face a very uphill struggle. Experienced IT professionals have a far better chance of securing work. For such people, finding work is not so much the problem. Overseas employers openly welcome UK IT staff. The problem in some cases is that of being *allowed* to work. Many countries outside the EU actively enforce visa controls, work permit regulations and other 'barriers', all of which the IT professional must negotiate and overcome. In addition, some countries are far more sensitive to academic qualifications than are the UK and most EU countries.

HAVING THE RIGHT COMPUTING SKILLS TO WORK ABROAD

Happily for us, the skills shortages abroad are strikingly similar to the skills shortage in the UK. Much the same IT skills are in short supply abroad as they are here.

Therefore, the skills currently in short supply and listed in Figure 4 are also the ones likely to be in demand abroad. A few specific countries of the world deviate from this general rule but, on the whole, there is no need to conduct detailed IT job market research for every country you are interested in working in. You can safely assume that, if the skill is in demand in the UK, it already is or will shortly be in demand overseas too.

Later in this chapter there is a country by country listing of the skills currently in shortest supply in each specific country.

FINDING AND APPLYING FOR A COMPUTING JOB ABROAD

How does someone go about finding and applying for computing work abroad? There are several methods and these are listed in order of preference and chances of success:

1. Using specialised computer recruitment agencies.
2. Using the UK Employment Service (see chapter 3).
3. Consulting specialised UK and foreign newspapers, magazines and journals.

There are other methods too, like writing speculative letters to foreign IT employers, contacting foreign embassies and Chambers of Commerce, contacting foreign recruitment agencies, and making appointments to meet potential employers whilst on holiday, for example. However, for computer professionals, these methods will only occasionally lead to full time work.

Contacting specialising computer recruitment agencies

This is by far the most fruitful method by which experienced computer professionals are able to secure work abroad. There are many UK based computer recruitment agencies specialising in finding work for suitably skilled, experienced and qualified computer professionals abroad. A selection is listed, together with the countries they specialise in recruiting for, in the Useful Addresses section.

Many deal solely within the EU or have a specific and limited number of countries in which they specialise.

Applying for IT jobs abroad through a recruitment agency is done in the same way as in the UK. The normal method is to send the agency an up-to-date copy of your CV, tailored to appeal to foreign computer employers, together with an informative covering letter stating where you would like to work, the kind of role you are hoping to secure and an indication of the level of salary you would hope to receive for your services. A typical covering letter is shown in Figure 15.

On receiving your covering letter and CV the recruitment agency, or preferably agencies, you have selected, will immediately attempt to match your skills and experience with current overseas vacancies.

Once you have indicated your interest in a particular position, the agency will contact the foreign employer with your details. If all goes well, an interview will be arranged.

Depending on the country you wish to work in, either the interview will be held abroad (typically the case for interviews in EU countries) or, if further afield like the USA, Canada, Australia or New Zealand, at agency premises or at the offices of a British or European subsidiary. This is to save expensive long haul air fares and to generally minimise employers' recruitment costs.

For most foreign appointments where interviews are conducted abroad, you can expect the recruitment agency to make and finalise all interview arrangements. Similarly the agency or the employer will normally bear the *whole* cost of all your air fares, hotel accommodation, train, taxi and other incurred expenses. Be extremely wary if you are ever asked to bear these costs.

Handling telephone interviews

Where standard face to face interviews are not possible, telephone interviews will be arranged by the agency. You will normally be telephoned by the employer rather than the other way around, though time zone differences could result in you being called late at night or early in the morning. A suitably convenient time will

Computer Recruitment Agency Ltd,, 31 Agency Road, London SW1 5FD.	8 Treetop Close Lower Westbury London SW1 1QW Tel: (0171) 123 4567 (days) Tel: (0171) 123 5555 (eves) 19 September 199X

Dear Sir,

Application for Permanent or Temporary Computer Work Overseas

Please find enclosed a fully up to date copy of my Curriculum Vitae and a passport sized photograph. I wish to be considered for computer programming or software engineering positions **anywhere in Europe** but preferably in **Holland, France** or **Germany. English is my first language** and I am also **fluent in German**.

My main skill areas are:

• **Unix (AIX, Ultrix)**	(3 years' experience)
• **Oracle Version 7 4GL, Forms, SQL**	(3 years)
• **'C'**	(5 years)
• **Powerbuilder 4.0**	(15 months)

I also have specific industry knowledge of:

• **Financial settlement systems**	(2 years)
• **Banking and insurance sectors**	(4 years)
• **Commodities trading and dealing systems**	(6 years)

My preference is for **ORACLE work** in some kind of **financial** or **insurance** background, though I would consider working in other industry areas.

I am single, mobile, a full UK passport and driving licence holder and am available at **two weeks' notice**. I can be available for interview at short notice and look forward to hearing from you shortly.

Yours faithfully

A. Eurohopeful Esq

Fig. 15. A sample covering letter to an agency specialising in computer jobs overseas.

have been prearranged by the agency—so you will not receive a call out of the blue.

Telephone interviews are likely to last between ten minutes and a couple of hours in some cases. Expect to be asked a whole range of questions covering technical computing subjects, detailed questions about your skills, background, experience and qualifications, and also searching questions centring around why you want to work abroad and particularly why you want to work in the employer's country.

Speaking the right language

As previously mentioned, English is often the language of first or second choice in most of the countries traditionally known to offer the most IT job opportunities to UK nationals. Your agency will specifically let you know if proficiency in a foreign language is necessary—because, more than likely, it will be a requirement of the employer.

If your agency does not mention language proficiency, then you can assume English is acceptable. However, if in doubt, a quick call to the agency will put your mind at ease.

All interviews, face to face or by telephone, will be conducted in English—unless previously notified and agreed. Most agency documentation and informative literature will also be in English —unless a foreign agency has been approached.

What to do after the interview

Computer recruitment agencies in the UK dealing with overseas vacancies are popular with both UK computer professionals and foreign employers because they provide a **full** service. As well as submitting CVs and job applications, arranging, paying for and possibly also accompanying candidates to interviews, in most cases agencies also offer a comprehensive immigration and advice service to candidates about to embark on their overseas career. This includes advising on passport and work permit applications, making travel arrangements on your behalf, securing your first few weeks' accommodation and advising on such things as local customs, local financial and taxation regulations, and a whole range of other highly applicable considerations.

It does not end there either. Once abroad, you can expect the agency to be in regular touch with you, possibly to put you in touch with other UK nationals or just to check all is going well.

Once you are established abroad, you may also be asked by your agency to help or assist others making the same journey.

Consulting newspapers, magazines and trade journals

A regular source of overseas jobs abroad are the national quality dailies such as:

- *The Daily Telegraph*
- *The Times*
- *The Guardian.*

In addition, *Computer Weekly* and *Computing* both carry a multitude of advertisements for computer opportunities abroad. These are invariably placed by the specialising computer recruitment agencies we have already discussed. However, some are also placed by overseas computer recruitment agencies hoping to attract UK nationals to specific countries—USA, Australia and New Zealand based agencies being the most common in this respect.

Some of the larger UK based recruitment agencies have specialised international divisions dedicated to finding skilled individuals work abroad. Some of these are listed at the back of the book.

Two more general jobs newspapers can also be used to seek computer work abroad:

- *Overseas Jobs Express*
  Island Publishing
  PO Box 22 Brighton BN1 6HX.
  Tel: (01273) 440220.

- *Home and Away*
  Expats International
  29 Lacon Road
  London SE22 9HE.
  Tel: (0181) 299 4986.

Although these papers contain many different types of job vacancies, computer opportunities are regularly in abundance. These papers also contain a wealth of information, local knowledge, practical advice and tips to individuals hoping to find and apply for work abroad.

Using foreign newspapers and journals

UK citizens are just as entitled to apply for jobs advertised in foreign journals as foreign nationals are for British ones. The major drawback here is the language barrier. Particularly:

- to read and understand the adverts in foreign newspapers and magazines, you need to be reasonably proficient in the language
- the job itself, as it is being advertised in a foreign language, is likely to necessitate fluency in that language during the day to day course of the job.

Most of the major European newspapers and magazines are widely available, or can be ordered, from larger newsagents. Expect cover prices to be higher though, sometimes much higher than they would be in their home country.

Producing Euro and overseas friendly CVs

It is almost unheard of to apply for computer related work overseas without having prepared a **detailed CV**. When preparing an overseas friendly CV, take your existing UK specific CV and:

- Ensure all addresses including your home, school, university and work addresses include the country name as well as all other details.
- Always quote your international telephone dialling code. For example, +44 171 999 999 where the '+' represents the caller's international dialling code, the '44' is the UK's international code and the '171' is, in this example, London's dialling code without the initial '0' with the rest of the number being your own telephone number.
- Avoid using abbreviations that may not be known abroad. Specify for example 'VISUAL BASIC' and 'Bachelor of Arts' rather than 'VB' and 'BA'.
- Specify in full the level of fluency you have in all foreign languages.

- Always include your nationality now and at birth.
- Ensure you include all names you are known under, including all middle names and any maiden names.
- Do include the full names and addresses of at least two referees.
- Do include a passport sized colour photograph of yourself.
- Consider including some information about how you came to hear of the vacancy.
- Number and staple pages in the correct order.
- Ask before sending the CV, but be prepared to include photocopies (originals in some cases) of important documents such as birth and marriage certificates, and certificates recording your academic or professional qualifications.

Remember that for overseas computing vacancies requiring fluency in a foreign language, you might be obliged to produce your CV in that language rather than in English.

Further reading

Getting Computer Jobs Abroad (CW Profession Series 1995) is available at £12.95 from Computer Weekly Publications, PO Box 935, Finchingfield, Braintree, Essex CM7 4LN. Tel: (0371) 811160.

COMPUTING OPPORTUNITIES—A COUNTRY BY COUNTRY GUIDE

For completeness, a country by country guide is given to include some of the more important aspects and information of concern to individuals searching for computer related work overseas. Countries are listed alphabetically and, although not all countries of the world are listed, the main ones known to offer a range of computer opportunities to UK nationals are included.

AUSTRALIA

General information

Traditionally a popular destination for emigrating British subjects. However, until very recently, the economic recession Australia has been experiencing meant that finding and then taking up IT work has been quite difficult. Happily the situation is now markedly easing.

Although the country is English speaking and uses much the same computer hardware and software as is used in the UK, to work in Australia UK nationals need to obtain a visa. Support and sponsorship from an Australian employer is also mandatory for any jobs lasting between four months and four years. In addition, candidates must also be able to offer computing skills recognised to be in short supply in Australia and must also meet certain personal and health criteria. For jobs likely to last longer than four years the requirements are even tougher.

Major locations of computing work
Melbourne, Sydney, Perth, Adelaide. Major cities.

Preferred languages
English.

Computing skills in demand
Mainly software related including 'C/C++', Unix Oracle and Ingres, Sybase, COBOL.

Living conditions
Comparable to UK. Property less expensive, cars more expensive.

Working conditions
40 hour working week, holiday entitlement broadly in line with UK.

Salary level vis a vis UK
Slightly less than UK for comparable work.

Work/residence permits
See general information above.

Useful addresses

Australian High Commission, Australia House, The Strand, London WC2B 4LA. Tel: (0171) 379 4334.

Further reading

How to Live and Work in Australia, L Veltman (How To Books 1996).

How to Get a Job in Australia, N Vandome (How To Books 1995).

The Australia and New Zealand Employment Guide (Overseas Employment Services).

Graduate Outlook, Hobsons Press, 491 Kent Street, Sydney, New South Wales 2000, Australia.

Looking for a Job (an Australian version of *The Graduate Post*) available by writing to GCC of Australia, PO Box 28, Parkville, Victoria, Australia.

FRANCE

General information

Many computing vacancies exist in France for suitably qualified and skilled professionals across a range of computing jobs, but particularly in the areas of software development and support. Though English is occasionally spoken within the confines of international computing companies, expect to have or to be asked to learn quickly to speak fluent French.

Major locations of computing work

Paris (many opportunities particularly in the computing departments of large international banks and financial institutions), Provence.

Preferred languages

French strongly preferred, occasionally German or English.

Computing skills in demand

Similar to UK but must usually be complemented by a detailed knowledge of particular industry sectors such as finance or manufacturing.

Living conditions
Good, daily costs lower than UK. Property in Paris can be very expensive to buy/rent. Elsewhere rates are slightly lower than UK.

Working conditions
In line with UK, though holiday entitlement is slightly higher at around five to six weeks per year. Taxation rates slightly higher (30%) on average than UK (25%).

Salary level vis a vis UK
Broadly similar to UK—Paris based work is paid for at roughly equivalent rates to London based work.

Work/residence permits
No work permit required. A temporary residence permit must be applied for within three months.

Useful address
French Embassy, 58 Knightsbridge, London SW1X 7JT. Tel: (0171) 235 8080.

Further reading

How To Live and Work in France, Nicole Prevost Logan (How To Books 1993).
Le Monde and *Le Figaro*—French quality newspapers commonly available from larger newsagents.

GERMANY

General information

Unified Germany, and particularly Western Germany, is known for its high standards of living, its willingness to import foreign labour (around seven per cent of all Germany's computing positions are filled with non-native Germans), and is particularly known to value the skills of British computer professionals.

Job opportunities abound in Germany—especially for skilled software engineers and for individuals skilled in installing configuring and operating computer communications hardware, networking software and telecommunications equipment.

Though English is more widely spoken as a second language

than in France, UK nationals should consider learning the German language as it is the preferred language within most German computing companies.

Major locations of computing work
All major cities in the former West Germany.

Preferred languages
German, English.

Computing skills in demand
Similar to UK but with an emphasis on telecommunications and networking hardware and software. Individuals are expected to have a very high level of appropriate skills and experience. Those with limited experience stand no chance.

Living conditions
West German living conditions are excellent—much better than the UK in most regions. Daily and property costs significantly higher than in UK.

Working conditions
Very good. A 40 hour working week, up to 42 days holiday a year. No active trade unions in the computer industry.

Salary level vis a vis UK
Between one and up to two times higher than UK.

Work/residence permits
No work permit required. A temporary residence permit must be applied for within three months.

Useful addresses
German Embassy, 23 Belgrave Square, London SW1X 0PZ. Tel: (0171) 235 5033.
The Employment Service, Overseas Placing Unit, 4th Floor, Steel City House, c/o Moorfoot, Sheffield S1 4PQ. Tel: (01742) 596051/2 (many German based computing jobs available).
German State Employment Service—very helpful and efficient with helping suitably skilled foreigners find more specialised

work such as computing: ZAV, Feuerbachstrasse 42, D-6000 Frankfurt/Main.

German Chamber of Industry and Commerce, 16 Buckingham Gate, London SW1E 6LB. Tel: (0171) 233 5656.

Further reading

How To Live and Work in Germany, Christine Hall (How To Books 1995).

How To Get a Job in Germany, Christine Hall (How To Books 1994).

Die Welt, Frankfurter Allgemeine—German newspapers offering a wide selection of vacancies—on sale or available on order from most leading UK newsagents.

HOLLAND

General information

For UK nationals, Holland is the most fertile source of IT and computing vacancies in the EU (outside of the UK). Traditionally Holland and the UK have maintained strong commercial and economic links, and for UK citizens in search of computer work abroad, Holland is perhaps the easiest country in which to secure work. English is widely spoken in Holland and normally there is no requirement to learn Dutch.

Major locations of computing work

All major cities in Holland, particularly Amsterdam and Rotterdam.

Preferred languages

English, very occasionally Dutch.

Computing skills in demand

Similar to UK but with an emphasis on telecommunications and networking hardware and software.

Living conditions

Living conditions are good, slightly better than most regions of the UK. Daily and property costs again slightly higher than in UK.

Working conditions
Good. A 38 hour working week, 15–21 days holiday per year. Taxation rates higher than in UK (15–70%).

Salary level vis a vis UK
Between 1 and 1.25 times higher than UK.

Work/residence permits
No work permit required. A temporary residence permit must be applied for within eight days of arrival in Holland.

Useful addresses
Royal Netherlands Embassy, 38 Hyde Park Gate, London SW7 5DP. Tel: (0171) 584 5040.
The Employment Service, Overseas Placing Unit, 4th Floor, Steel City House, c/o Moorfoot, Sheffield S1 4PQ. Tel: (01742) 596051/2.
Dutch State Employment Services—very helpful with helping suitably skilled foreigners find more specialised work such as computing: Single 202, 1016 Amsterdam. Tel: 020 520 0911.

Further reading

Intermedair. A weekly jobs newspaper published by Uitgevertj Intermediaire, Postbus, 3434 1001 AE Amsterdam, Holland—available on order from larger UK newsagents.

IRELAND (Republic of)

General information

Traditionally seen as a country from which people emigrate to find work, the Republic of Ireland has consequently been left with significant skills shortages—notably in computing and other high technology industries. English is spoken almost universally and British workers are both commonplace and welcome—especially in areas such as telecommunications and software development roles.

Major locations of computing work
Dublin, Cork.

Preferred languages
English.

Computer skills in demand
Same as UK.

Living conditions
Same/slightly better than UK. Daily and property costs again slightly higher than in UK.

Working conditions
Broadly comparable to UK, though taxation rates are higher (35–60%) and holiday entitlement slightly lower at around 18–20 days.

Salary level vis a vis UK
Comparable to UK.

Work/residence permits
No work permit required, though British citizens working in the Republic of Ireland are required to hold a full UK passport.

Useful addresses
Embassy of the Republic of Ireland, 17 Grosvenor Place, London SW1X 7HR. Tel: (0171) 235 2171.
The Employment Service, Overseas Placing Unit, 4th Floor, Steel City House, c/o Moorfoot, Sheffield S1 4PQ. Tel: (01742) 596051/2 (a few Irish based computing jobs available).
A list of Irish employment agencies which can be contacted directly by UK computer staff is available from: The Department of Labour, 65a Adelaide Road, Dublin 2, Republic of Ireland.

Most major UK computer agencies deal with computer vacancies in the Republic of Ireland which for practical purposes are resourced and treated in the same way as those within the UK.

Further reading
Irish newspapers advertising computer jobs include the *Irish Independent* which publishes most computer job vacancies on Thursdays, *The Irish Times* (Fridays) and *The Irish Press* (Thursdays). All are on sale or can be ordered from leading UK newsagents.

NEW ZEALAND

General information

The New Zealand government retains strong links with the UK and is on the whole seen as being more 'pro British' than Australia. Traditionally, New Zealand has welcomed skilled and experienced UK nationals to fill the computing vacancies it cannot fill with local people, and opportunities are still quite good. However, entry into New Zealand for the purposes of finding work is no longer so easy. Individual New Zealand based employers must first satisfy the local Department of Labour that a vacant IT post cannot be filled by a local person. When and if a visa is granted, it is normally only valid for three years.

New Zealand now assesses its immigrants on a points system. This system is based on academic qualifications, previous work experience and age.

Major locations of computing work
Wellington, Auckland.

Preferred languages
English.

Computing skills in demand
Mainly software related including 'C/C++', Unix Oracle and Ingres, Sybase, COBOL, Progress, Paradox, Foxbase.

Living conditions
Comparable to UK. Property less expensive, cars more expensive.

Working conditions
40 hour working week, holiday entitlement broadly in line with UK.

Salary level vis a vis UK
Slightly less than UK for comparable work.

Work/residence permits
See general information above.

Useful addresses

New Zealand High Commission, New Zealand House, 80 Haymarket, London SW1Y 4TQ. Tel: (0171) 930 8422.

Michael Green, Aacorn International Ltd. Box 105–355, Auckland Central, New Zealand. Tel: +64 9 309 7862; Fax: +64 9 309 9043—a well known IT recruitment organisation specialising in finding Europeans and UK nationals IT posts in New Zealand.

Further reading

How to Live and Work in New Zealand, J Muirhead (How To Books 1995).

New Zealand Herald—the foremost newspaper in New Zealand. Contact New Zealand Associated Press, 107 Fleet Street, London EC4A 2AN.

SWITZERLAND

General information

Switzerland is one of the most glamorous and prosperous countries of Europe. Though not an EU member, Switzerland focuses much of its effort on developing high technology such as computerised telecommunications, communications software and a range of other types of computer software, products and services. Most Swiss product and software development is designed to support its traditionally strong banking, financial and insurance sectors. The Swiss are always happy to recruit British and British trained computer professionals, all of whom enjoy an enviable reputation there. In addition, Swiss prosperity means that in general employers can afford to pay very high rates to those with the highest levels of specialist skills and experience.

Switzerland is currently experiencing a severe shortage of certain computer skills. However, the problem is not so much finding work in the Swiss IT industry as being allowed to work there. A valid work permit is required as is a good knowledge of either French or German in most cases. The Swiss normally go to some lengths to ensure they recruit only the highest calibre of computer staff and very often it is strongly advisable for UK professionals to have located work in Switzerland before leaving the UK.

Major locations of computing work
Geneva, Zurich, Berne.

Preferred languages
French and German, English.

Computing skills in demand
Same as UK but with a strong emphasis on lower level programming languages such as 'C' and assembler. Also, computer networking, communications and telecommunications skills are in short supply. Knowledge of databases such as Ingres, Sybase and Oracle are useful if these are also supplemented by a strong knowledge of the banking, financial or insurance industry.

Living conditions
Some of the best anywhere in the world. Daily and property costs very high—up to three times higher than the UK.

Working conditions
38 hour week on average. 30 days per year holiday. Taxation levels higher than UK.

Salary level vis a vis UK
Up to three times as high as UK

Work/residence permits
Both work and residence permits may be required. Check with Swiss Embassy as current permit regulations are changing.

Useful address
Swiss Embassy, 16–18 Montagu Place, London W1H 2BQ. Tel: (0171) 723 0701.

Further reading

Le Journal de l'Emploi—a Swiss professional and executive jobs newspaper available from *Le Journal de l'Emploi*, 20 Place Cornavin, 1202 Geneva, Switzerland.

Employment for British Subjects in Switzerland—produced by The British Embassy, Thunstrasse 50, 3000 Berne, Switzerland.

Living and Working in Switzerland, D Hampshire (Survival Books).

USA

General information

The USA is the home base of the world's largest and most powerful computer manufacturers and software companies. The USA is so big and offers so many different computing opportunities that many of the specialised computer recruitment agencies in the UK deal only with vacancies in the USA. Some agencies restrict their area of operations even further—to specific areas of the USA such as California and Silicon Valley.

Again, the British computer professional is highly regarded in the USA and a wealth of computer opportunities exists there. So much so in fact that a considerable 'brain drain' has been experienced by the UK and Europe, which have lost many of their highest ranking technical IT specialists to the USA.

However, again the problem is that of being allowed to work in the country. To qualify for computer related work, individuals are required to have a recognised UK university degree or at least two or three years' demonstrable computing experience. Once this has been proved, a complex system of non immigrant visas (those issued to individuals seeking temporary work in the USA) has to be negotiated, and an appropriate visa obtained before even being allowed to enter the county. Immigrant visas, issued to individuals wanting to work permanently in the USA, are not easy to obtain.

Major locations of computing work
California/all major cities.

Preferred languages
English.

Computing skills in demand
Same as UK but with a strong emphasis on relational database skills such as Oracle and Sybase. Unix, COBOL, CICS, SQL and C/C++ also in demand.

Living conditions
Very good. Daily costs lower than UK. Property prices vary greatly depending on location.

Working conditions
40 hour week on average. 15–20 days' holiday per year. Taxation levels generally lower than UK.

Salary level vis a vis UK
Slightly lower on average.

Work/residence permits
Complex system of non-immigrant/immigrant visa to be negotiated. Unless entering the country on holiday, a visa will be a prerequisite before you will be allowed into the country. Visas can usually only be obtained once work has already been secured.

Useful addresses
US Embassy, 124 Grosvenor Square, London W1A 2JB. Tel: (0171) 499 9000.
US Visa Branch, 5 Upper Grosvenor Street, London W1A 2JB. Tel: (0171) 499 3443.
Most major UK computer recruitment agencies have sections dealing with computer vacancies in the USA. A list of such agencies and their addresses is given in the Useful Addresses section.

Further reading

How To Live and Work in America, Steve Mills (How To 1995).
How To Get a Job in America, Roger Jones (How To 1994).
Applying for a US Visa, R Fleisher (International Venture Handbooks 1993).

OTHER COUNTRIES

The following is a list of other countries together with typical computing skills currently in demand by them. Many computer job opportunities exist in these countries, though for some reason they appear not to be that well covered by many of the UK's larger computer recruitment agencies.

Canada

Usual skills required. C/C++, Unix, relational databases and currently a fairly strong requirement for COBOL and CICS programmers. Contact Computer People International, Piccadilly House, 33 Regent Street, London W1Y 4NB. Tel: (0171) 287 0050; Fax: (0171) 287 0785 and ask about their Canadian vacancies.

Saudi Arabia and Kuwait

Have had many IT positions on offer in the past. There seem to be fewer nowadays. Requirements include COBOL, CICS, PL/1, Unix, ORACLE. Contact LA International Computer Consultants, Ridge House, Ridge House Drive, Festival Park, Stoke on Trent ST1 5SJ. Tel: (01782) 279099; Fax: (01782) 273919.

Japan

The world's second largest computer market. Opportunities for highly skilled, highly experienced (5 years+) computing professionals have always been abundant, though for some reason not particularly well covered by UK computer recruitment agencies. Skills in demand include C/C++, the currently trendy ORACLE and SYBASE relational databases and Unix, MS-DOS and telecommunications software and hardware. Knowledge of the Japanese language is normally a prerequisite. Salaries, as well as Japan's standard of living, can be very high. Contact Computer People International, Piccadilly House, 33 Regent Street, London W1Y 4NB. Tel: (0171) 287 0050; Fax: (0171) 287 0785 and ask about their Japanese vacancies. Or contact Spencer Stuart Japan Ltd, who specialise in placing IT professionals in Japan, at Ark Mori Building, 1-12-32 Akasaka, Tokyo 107, Japan. Tel: (03) 3505-4571.

Appendix A

Answers to example aptitude test questions and worked explanations

1. What is the next number in the sequence: 1, 3, 5, 7, 11, 13, 17 . . . ?
   Answer 19. Next in the series of prime numbers (those divisible only by themselves and 1).

2. What is the next letter in the sequence: W T F S S M . . . ?
   Answer T. Starting with (W)ednesday, all represent the first letters of the days of the week in order. T = Tuesday.

3. What is the next word in the sequence: bit byte kilobyte . . . ?
   Answer Megabyte. The next unit of measurement of computer memory or data size.

4. Complete the following: Black is to white as night is to . . .
   Answer Day—the opposite of night, just as white is the opposite of black.

5. A man got into a lift on the bottom floor of a 100 storey building. As the lift was rising the man exclaimed 'I've missed my floor. The floor I wanted to get off on is 15 more than the square root of the floor I am now on.' Since the man was just less than half way up the building what floor was he currently on and what floor did he really want to get off at?
   Answer Currently on floor 49. He should have got off on floor 22. We are told that the man is just less than half way up the building of 100 floors. Since the floors of buildings are whole numbers (floor 1, 2, 3, 4 and so on) the square root of a number slightly under 50 must give a whole number. Looking at the

squares of numbers starting at 1, 4, 9, 16, 25, 36, 49, we see that floor 49 is slightly less half way up the 100 floor building. So this is the floor the man is currently on. The square root of 49 is 7. Add 15 to this to give 22—the floor the man had wanted to get off at, but missed.

Glossary

Analysis. The study of business problems or customer requirements.

Application. A computer program used for a particular purpose or kind of work—like word processing, for example.

Back up. An additional copy of your software and data in case the information on your computer is lost or becomes unusable.

Bug. An error in a computer program.

Bulletin board. An on-line information service, available to all computer users with a modem.

CD-ROM. A round silvery disk capable of storing huge quantities of information and which can be inserted into a computer.

Commands. Instructions input into a computer by a user which cause the computer to perform a desired action—like 'copy' a file or 'list' several files.

Computer. A machine for running software.

Consultancy. Giving specialist advice to others usually on business problems.

CV. Your personal history written up to present to employers or others.

Database. A collection of information.

Design. A plan for constructing a piece of software.

Device. A piece of computer equipment.

Disk. A thin circular flat plate, coated with a magnetic film which is used to store information and data.

Disk drive. A device used for reading information from and writing information to computer disks.

Electronic mail (e-mail). A system for sending and receiving messages from one computer to another via a modem.

File. A named collection of information held together and stored on magnetic disk, tape or compact disk.

Floppy disk. A small round magnetic disk capable of being inserted into a computer and which carries information.

Hard disk. A magnetic device located inside a computer used for storing information.

Hardware. A term covering all forms of computer equipment—such as processors, hard disks, circuit boards, printers, monitors and keyboards.

Information technology (IT). The use of computers and other electronic and telecommunications technology to manipulate, store and transfer information.

Internet. A popular on-line information service allowing access to the information held on computers all over the world.

Joystick. A piece of equipment often used by computer games players to steer or control images on the screen.

Language. A set of commands which can be used to write computer programs. Examples of some computer languages are: BASIC, 'C', COBOL, PASCAL.

Mainframe. A very large computer used for processing huge quantities of data and supporting large numbers of computer terminals.

Memory. A temporary storage area inside a computer that is used to hold applications and data.

Microcomputer. A small computer of the kind commonly used in schools, offices and homes.

Minicomputer. A larger computer, typically used to process fairly substantial amounts of computer data and usually supporting a number of different computer terminals linked to it.

Modem. A device enabling one computer to communicate with another.

Monitor. Another word for a computer screen.

Mouse. A hand operated device used to control a computer.

Network. A system for linking computers together or for linking computer terminals and screens to a central computer.

Printer. A device used for producing printed material.

Processor. A device inside a computer used for executing computer programs.

Program. A series of computer instructions which together cause the computer to perform a specified task.

Programming. The act of assembling computer instructions so that together they cause the computer to perform a specified task.

RAM. An acronym for Random Access Memory. Information and applications are stored temporarily in memory of this type. They are lost if the computer is switched off.

Requirements. Tasks people want a software package to handle.

Scanner. A device for transferring images and text from paper and other mediums onto a computer.

Scrolling. Movements (left, right, up, down) of the image displayed on screen.

Software. A collection of one or more computer programs.

Software development. See 'Programming'.

Telephone support. A facility provided by software suppliers which allows their software users to telephone for help or advice.

Terminal. A computer screen or VDU linked to a computer network.

Testing. The process of checking software to ensure it works as expected.

VDU (Visual Display Unit). A common name for any computer screen on which data is displayed.

Word processor. A computer program which can be used to write letters, reports or other documents.

Further Reading

COMPUTER TRADE NEWSPAPERS AND MAGAZINES

Computing (VNU Business Publications)—a weekly IT newspaper distributed to IT professionals on application to The Circulation Manager, *Computing*, VNU Business Publications, VNU House, 32–34 Broadwick Street, London W1A 2HG. Tel: (0171) 316 9000; Fax: (0171) 316 9160.

Computer Weekly (Reed Business Publishing)—a weekly IT newspaper distributed to IT professionals on application to The Circulation Manager, *Computer Weekly*, Quadrant House, The Quadrant, Sutton, Surrey SM2 5AS. Tel: (01444) 441212; Fax: (01444) 445588.

Personal Computer Magazine (VNU)—trade magazine with a bias towards reporting on PC related issues. Does not usually carry job advertisements. Available on subscription from VNU Business Publications, VNU House, 32–34 Broadwick Street, London W1A 2HG. Tel: (0171) 316 9000; Fax: (0171) 316 9160.

MAGAZINES FOR THE FREELANCE IT PROFESSIONAL

Freelance Informer, available to all existing computer freelancers and to those considering contracting as a career. Published fortnightly and available on application to The Circulation Manager, *Freelance Informer*, Quadrant House, The Quadrant, Surrey SM2 5AS or by telephoning the *Freelance Informer* help line (01753) 567567.

Computer Contractor, available to all existing computer freelancers and to those considering contracting as a career. Published fortnightly and available on application to The Circulation Manager, *Computer Contractor*, VNU Business Publications,

32–34 Broadwick Street, London W1A 2HG or by telephoning the circulation hot line (0171) 316 9700.

WRITING A CV

The Perfect CV, Max Eggert (Century 1992).
How To Write a CV That Works, Paul McGee (How To Books 1995).

COMPUTER TRAINING BOOKS

The following selection of books has been chosen as the ones most likely to provide you with the computer skills/knowledge of most use and in most demand by employers at the current time.

DATABASES

Fundamentals Of Database Systems, Elmasri and Navathe (Addison Wesley 1994).
Introduction to Database Systems, C Date (Addison Wesley 1995).
The Relational Database, J Carter (Chapman & Hall 1995).
Beginner's Guide to Access 2.0 (Wrox Press 1994).
How To Use Microsoft Access (2.0), Eric Stone (Ziff-Davis Press 1994).
Understanding DBASE V for Windows, A Simpson (Sybex 1995).
Understanding SQL, Elizabeth Lynch (Macmillan).
A Guide to DB2, Date and White (Addison Wesley 1992).
Running Microsoft FoxPro for Windows, S Riccciardi (Microsoft Press 1993).
Introduction to Ingres, L Zinky (PWS 1992).
Oracle: The Complete Reference, G Kock (McGraw Hill 1995).
Oracle 7: A Users and Developers Guide, G Sturner (International Thompson 1995).
Teach Yourself Paradox 5 For Windows (MIS Press).
Sybase Developers Guide (SAMS 1994).
Sybase Architecture and Administration, J Kirkwood (Ellis Horwood 1993).
Programming Informix—A step by step approach, C Kipp (Prentice-Hall 1994).
Informix 4GL Tutorial, Mahler (Prentice-Hall).

NETWORKING AND COMMUNICATIONS

How To Use the Internet, Jones (How To Books 1996).
CC: Mail Plain and Simple, C Rennie (Sybex 1994).
Client Server Computing, Smith and Patrick (SAMS 1994).
Novell's Guide To Client Server Applications and Architecture, J Schank (Sybex 1994).
Communications and Networking for the PC, Jordan & Churchill (NRP 1994).
Dvorak's Guide to PC Telecommunications, J Dvorak (McGraw Hill 1992).
The Complete Communications Book, E Paulson (Wordware 1992).
The E-Mail Companion, J Quarterman (Addison Wesley 1994).
E-Mail—A Practical Guide, S Collin (CW Professional Series 1995).
Internet: The Complete Reference (McGraw Hill 1993).
Internet With Windows, Glyn Moody (CW Professional Series 1995).
Lotus Notes Application Development (IDG Books 1995).
Lotus Notes—A Practical Guide, S Collin (CW Professional Series 1995).
Modems Made Easy, D Hakala (McGraw Hill 1993).
Novell Netware 4.0: The Complete Reference, T Sheldon (McGraw Hill 1993).
Absolute Beginners Guide To Networking, M Gibbs (SAMS 1994).
Build Your Own Computer Accessories, B Hargreaves (Windcrest 1993).
Interfacing to the IBM Personal Computer, C Eggebrecht (SAMS).
Windows Programmer's Guide to Serial Communications, T Monk (SAMS 1992).
X.25 Made Easy, N Thorpe (Prentice Hall 1992).

OPERATING SYSTEMS

CICS—Command Level Programming (Wiley).
Peter Norton's DOS 6.22 Guide, Peter Norton (SAMS 1995).
The Official Guide to OS/2 Warp, R Stagray (IDG Books 1995).
Unix Commands by Example, D Elboth (Prentice Hall 1994).
Unix System V Release 4—An Introduction (Osborne/McGraw Hill 1994).

Teach Yourself (Unix) Shell Programming in 14 Days, K Husain (SAMS 1994).
Insiders Guide to Windows 95 Programming, F Houlette (Que 1995).
Windows 95 Programming in C and C+ +, Herb Schildt (Osborne/McGraw Hill 1995).
Windows 95 Revealed, J Nimersham (Random House 1994).
Windows For Workgroups 3.11 in Easy Steps, H Kotecha (Computer Step 1994).
Windows NT: The Complete Reference, A Wyatt (Osborne/McGraw Hill 1993).
VMS Users Guide, J Peters (Digital Press).
AS400 Programming, B Coydon (McGraw Hill).

COMPUTER PROGRAMMING

Using ANSI C in Unix (Oxborne/McGraw-Hill 1990).
C Programming in a Unix Environment, K Kay (Prentice Hall).
Windows Made Simple, P McBride (Butterworth Heinemann 1994).
Programming in ADA, Trembley and Frieson (McGraw Hill).
Assembly Language Step by Step, J Duntermann (Wiley 1992).
Using Visual Basic: Writing Windows Applications, W Murray (Addison Wesley 1992).
Beginners Guide To Visual Basic, P Wright (Wrox 1994).
Teach Yourself More Visual Basic 4, P Perry (SAMS 1995).
The Visual Guide To Visual Basic For Windows, R Mansfield (Ventana 1993).
'C' The Complete Reference, H Schildt (Psborne/McGraw Hill 1995).
Teach Yourself 'C' in 21 Days, P Aitken (SAMS 1993).
'C+ +' The Complete Reference, H Schildt (Osborne/McGraw Hill 1995).
'C+ +' Programmers Handbook, P Lucas (Prentice Hall).
Teach Yourself Borland 'C+ +' in 21 Days, Amush (SAMS 1995).
Teach Yourself (Microsoft) C+ +, Holzgang (MIS Press 1995).
The Visual C+ + Handbook, C Pappas (Osborne/McGraw Hill 1994).
Essential Cobol, R Norman (McGraw Hill).
Teach Yourself Delphi, T Hall (MIS Press 1995).
Delphi By Example (Que 1995).
Mastering Pascal Programming, E Huggins (Macmillan 1993).

Developing Powerbuilder Applications, B Hatfield (SAMS 1994).
Powerbuilder 4: A Developers Guide, D McClanahan *M&T Publishing 1995).
How to Program Well, H Shapiro (Addison Wesley 1993).

SOFTWARE DESIGN METHODOLOGIES

An Introduction to SSADM Version 4, C Ashworth (McGraw Hill 1992).
SSADM Version 4: A Practical Approach, M Goodland (McGraw Hill 1992).
SSADM, C Bentley (CW Professional Series 1995).
Prince, K Bradley (CW Professional Series 1992).

MICROPROCESSORS

How Microprocessors Work, T Hammerstrom (Ziff Davis Press 1994).
Understanding Microprocessors, A Thompson (Delmar 1995).
Pentium Processor System Architecture, D Anderson (Mindshare 1994).
PowerPC, S Heath (CW Professional Series 1994).

HARDWARE MAINTENANCE GUIDES

Expand, Modernise and Repair PCs, R Penfold (Bernard- Babani).
Easy PC Maintenance and Repair, P Lalpante (Windcrest).
Computer Technicians Handbook, A Margolis (Windcrest).
PC Maintenance and Upgrade Guide, M Minasi (Sybex).
Build Your Own Pentium PC, A Pilgrim (Windcrest).
Easy Laser Printer Maintenance and Repair, S Bigelow (Windcrest).

OTHER

Running Word 6 (Microsoft Press 1995).
Running Excel 5 (Microsoft Press 1995).
PC Multimedia, F Botto (CW Professional Series 1994).
A full catalogue of books for the aspiring computer professional can be obtained by writing to: Computer Manuals, Freepost, 205 Formans Road, Sparkhill, Birmingham B11 2BA: Tel: (0121) 706 6000; Fax: (0121) 706 3301.

SELECTION OF COMPUTER TRAINING VIDEOS

Introduction to Windows 95
Advanced Guide to Windows 95
Programming in C++
Beginners Guide to DOS 6
Microsoft Word For Beginners
Microsoft Word Advanced
Microsoft Excel For Beginners
Microsoft Excel Advanced
Visual Basic For Beginners
and about 20 other titles, all available at under £20 from The Software Warehouse, The Gyratory, Hangar Lane, London W5 1EE. Tel: (0181) 810 7770 or (01675) 466 467.

Windows 3.1 Beginners Guide
Windows 3.1 Advanced Guide
OS/2 Warp Getting Started
Paradox For Windows
Access 2.0 Beginners
GoxPro 2.5 Beginners
C Programming
C++ Programming
Visual Basic
Netware 4.X Administration Vols 1 & 2
Lotus Notes Vols 1 & 2
Networking With Windows 95
Learning PC Fundamentals
Beginners Guide To PC Computers
Communicating With the Internet
plus around 190 other video titles all available from Burgess Video Group, Unit 18, Industrial Estate, Brecon, Powys LD3 8LA. Tel: (01874) 611633; Fax: (01874) 622994.

CD ROM BASED COMPUTER AIDED LEARNING (CAL) SOFTWARE

These interactive CD ROM based educational courses contain both video and sound to help you gain a grounding in the subject you have chosen. To run them you will need a compatible CD

ROM drive and an IBM compatible personal computer. Over 200 titles including at around £40 each:

Introduction to Excel
Introduction to Word
Introduction to Access
Learning Visual Basic
Programming in C
Programming in C+ +
Learning Windows 95
Professor DOS
Microsoft Office
Using the Internet
Further information from The Burgess Video Group, Unit 18, Industrial Estate, Brecon, Powys LD3 8LA. Tel: (01874) 611633; Fax: (01874) 622994.

RECRUITMENT DIRECTORIES

The International Recruitment Guide and Directory, Matthew Cunningham (International Venture Handbooks 1995).

CW IT Consultants Directory—annual publication listing UK consultancies, IT recruitment agencies, training organisations and computer services companies, available from The Marketing Department, Bowker-Saur, Maypole House, Maypole Road, East Grinstead, West Sussex TH19 1HH. Tel: (01342) 330100 or Fax: (01342) 330198.

Freelancer Informer Year Book—directory of computer recruitment agencies specialising in recruiting freelance IT professionals available from Quadrant House, The Quadrant, Surrey, SM2 5AS or by telephoning the *Freelance Informer* help line (01753) 567567.

CORRESPONDENCE COURSES ON COMPUTING

Free information from International Correspondence Schools, 312–314 High Street, Sutton, Surrey SM1 1PH or 8 Elliot Place, Clydeway Centre, Glasgow G3 8BR. Tel: (0141) 221 7373; Fax: (0141) 221 8151 on courses including programming in C and BASIC, Introduction to Programming, and specialist hardware related courses on PC assembly, repair and maintenance.

WORKING ABROAD/COMPUTING CAREERS ABROAD

Working on Contract Worldwide, Rod Briggs (How To Books 1996).
Working in the Gulf, Dr Hamid Atiyyah (International Venture Handbooks 1994).
Getting Computer Jobs Abroad (CW Professional Series 1995).

OVERSEAS JOBS NEWSPAPERS

Overseas Jobs Express, Island Publishing, PO Box 22, Brighton BN1 6HX. Tel: (01273) 440220. Fortnightly jobs newspaper with features on specific countries and overseas careers—IT and computing are particularly well catered for.
Home and Away, Expats International, 29 Lacon Road, London SE22 9HE. Tel: (0181) 299 4986. Monthly periodical covering overseas job vacancies.

Useful Addresses

GENERAL INFORMATION ON CAREERS IN COMPUTING

The British Computer Society, 13 Mansfield Street, London W1M 0BD. Tel: (0171) 637 0471.

Institute Of Data Processing Management, 21 Russell Street, London WC2B 5UB. Tel: (0171) 240 3305.

National Computing Centre, Oxford Road, Manchester M1 7ED. Tel: (0161) 228 6333; Fax: (0161) 228 2579.

Institution of Analysts and Programmers, Charles House, 36 Culmington Road, London W13 9NH. Tel: (0181) 567 2118; Fax: (0181) 567 4379.

SOME UK UNIVERSITIES OFFERING COMPUTER SCIENCE DEGREE COURSES FOR 1996–1997

University prospectuses detailing specific computer related courses on offer can be obtained by writing or telephoning the universities whose addresses and telephone numbers are given below.

Aberdeen University, Regent Walk, Aberdeen AB9 1FX. Tel: (01224) 272090; Fax: (01224) 276054.

Abertay University, Bell Street, Dundee DD1 1HG. Tel: (01382) 308080; Fax: (01382) 308877.

Aberystwyth University, Old College, King Street, Aberystwyth, Dyfed SY23 2AX. Tel: (01970) 622021; Fax: (01970) 627410.

Anglia Poly University, Victoria Road South, Chelmsford, Essex CM1 1LL. Tel: (01245) 493131.

Aston University, Aston Triangle, Birmingham, B4 7ET. Tel: (0121) 3593611; Fax: (0121) 3336350.

Belfast University, Queens University of Belfast, University Road, Belfast BT7 1NN. Tel: (01232) 245133; Fax: (01232) 247895.

Birmingham University, Edgbaston, Birmingham B15 2TT. Tel: (0121) 4143374; Fax: (0121) 4143971.

Bournemouth University, Talbot Campus, Fern Barrow, Poole, Dorset BH12 5BB. Tel: (01202) 524111; Fax: (01202) 513293.

Bradford University, Bradford, West Yorkshire BD7 1DP. Tel: (01274) 733466; Fax: (01274) 305340.

Brighton University, Lewes Road, Brighton, East Sussex BN2 4AT. Tel: (01273) 600900; Fax: (01273) 642607.

Bristol University, Senate House, Tyndall Avenue, Bristol BS8 1TH. Tel: (0117) 9289000; Fax: (0117) 9251424.

Bristol UWE, Frenchay Campus, Coldharbour Lane, Bristol BS16 1QY. Tel: (0117) 9656261; Fax: (0117) 9763804.

Brunel University, Uxbridge, Middlesex UB8 3PH. Tel: (01895) 274000; Fax: (01895) 203096.

Cambridge University, Cambridge CB2 1TN. Tel: (01223) 332200; Fax: (01223) 66383.

Cardiff Institute of Higher Education, Western Avenue, Llandaff, Cardiff CF5 2SG. Tel: (01222) 551111; Fax: (01222) 506911.

Coventry University, Priory Street, Coventry CV1 5FB. Tel: (01203) 631313; Fax: (01203) 838793.

Derby University, Kedleston Road, Derby DE22 1GB. Tel: (01332) 622222; Fax: (01332) 294861.

Dundee University, Dundee DD1 4HN. Tel: (01382) 223181; Fax: (01382) 221554.

Durham University, Old Shire Hall, Durham DH1 3HP. Tel: (0191) 374200; Fax: (0191) 3743740.

East Anglia University, Norwich, Norfolk NR4 7TJ. Tel: (01603) 456161; Fax: (01603) 458596.

Edinburgh University, Old College, South Bridge, Edinburgh EH8 9YL. Tel (0131) 6501000; Fax: (0131) 6684565.

Essex University, Wivenhoe Park, Colchester CO4 3SQ. Tel: (01206) 873333; Fax: (01206) 873423.

Glasgow Caledonian University, City Campus, Cowcaddens Road, Glasgow G4 0BA. Tel: (0141) 3313000; Fax: (0141) 3313005.

Heriot-Watt University, Riccarton, Edinburgh EH14 4AS. Tel: (0131) 449 5111.

Huddersfield University, Queensgate, Huddersfield HD1 3DH. Tel: (01484) 422288.

Hull University, Hull HU6 7RX. Tel: (01482) 46311; Fax: (01482) 465936.

Kent University, Canterbury, Kent CT2 7NZ. Tel: (01227) 764000.

Kingston University, Penrhyn Road, Kingston upon Thames KT1 2EE. Tel: (0181) 547 2000; Fax: (0181) 547 7093.

Leicester University, University Road, Leicester LE1 7RH. Tel: (0116) 2522522; Fax: (0116) 252 2447.

Liverpool John Moores University, Rodney House, 70 Mount Pleasant, Liverpool L3 5UX. Tel: (0151) 231 2121; Fax: (0151) 2313194.

Loughborough University of Technology, Loughborough, Leicestershire LE11 3TU. Tel: (01509) 263171; Fax: (01509) 219337.

Manchester University, Manchester M13 9PL. Tel: (0161) 2752000.

North London University, 166 Holloway Road, London N7 8DB. Tel: (0171) 6072789; Fax: (0171) 753 5075.

Portsmouth University, 1 Guildhall Walk, Portsmouth PO1 2RY. Tel: (01705) 876543.

Sheffield University, Western Bank, Sheffield S10 2TN. Tel: (0114) 276 8555; Fax: (0114) 272 8014.

South Bank University, Borough Road, London SE1 0AA. Tel: (0171) 928 8989; Fax: (0171) 815 6199.

Staffordshire University, College Road, Stoke-on-Trent ST4 2DE. Tel: (01782) 744531; Fax: (01782) 745422.

Strathclyde University, Glasgow G1 1XQ. Tel: (0141) 552 4400; Fax: (0141) 552 7362.

Sunderland University, Langham Tower, Ryhope Road, Sunderland SR2 7EE. Tel: (0191) 5152000; Fax: (0191) 515 2423.

Sussex University, Falmer, Brighton, Sussex BN1 9RH. Tel: (01273) 678416; Fax: (01273) 6784545.

Swansea Institute of Higher Education, Townhill Road, Swansea SA2 0UT. Tel: (01792) 481000; Fax: (01792) 208683.

UMIST, PO Box 88, Sackville Street, Manchester M60 1QD. Tel: (0161) 236 3311; Fax: (0161) 228 7040.

Warwick University, Coventry CV4 7AL. Tel: (01203) 523523; Fax: (01203) 461606.

Westminster University, 309 Regent Street, London W1R 8AL. Tel: (0171) 911 5000; Fax: (0171) 911 5118.

York University, Heslington, York YO1 5DD. Tel: (01904) 430000; Fax: (01904) 433433.

The Open University, Central Enquiry Service, PO Box 200, Walton Hall, Milton Keynes MK7 6YZ. Tel: (01908) 653231.

A SELECTION OF THE UK'S TOP IT COMPANIES

Admiral Computing Ltd, Admiral House, 193–199 London Road, Camberley, Surrey GU15 3JT. Tel: (01276) 692269.

Andersen Consulting, 2 Arundel Street, London WC2R 3LT. Tel: (0171) 438 5000.

Apple UK, 6 Roundwood Avenue, Stockley Park, Uxbridge, Middx UB11 1BB. Tel: (0181) 569 1199.

Apricot UK, 3500 Parkside, Birmingham Business Park, Birmingham B37 7YS. Tel: (0121) 717 7171.

AT&T Network Systems UK, Swindon Road, Malmesbury SN16 9NA. Fax: (01666) 832196.

BBC Recruitment Services, PO Box 7000, London W5 2WY. Tel: (0181) 849 0849.

Bull Information Systems, Computer House, Great West Road, Brentford, Middx TW8 9DH. Tel: (0181) 568 9191.

CMG, Telford House, Tothill Street, London SW1H 9NB. Tel: (0171) 233 0288.

Compaq Computers Ltd, Mitre House, Canbury Park Road, Kingston upon Thames Surrey KT2 6BR.

Data General, Data General Tower, Great West Road, Brentford, Middx TW3 9AN. Tel: (0181) 758 6000.

Data Sciences Ltd, Pinehurst House, Farnborough Road, Farnborough, Hants GU14 7NB. Tel: (01252) 544321.

DEC, PO Box 110, Reading, Berks RG2 0TR. Tel: (0800) 393200.

GEC MARCONI, Elstree Way, Borehamwood, Herts WD6 1RX. Tel: (0181) 732 0695; Fax: (0181) 732 0496.

Hewlett Packard, Cain Road, Bracknell, Berks RG12 1HN. Tel: (01344) 360000.

Hoskyns Group, Glen House, Stag Place, London SW1E 5AG. Tel: (0171) 830 6830.

IBM UK, The Recruitment Centre, PO Box 41, North Harbour, Portsmouth, Hants PO6 3AL. Tel: (01705) 561 500.

ICL, Waterside Park, Cain Road, Bracknell, Berks RG12 1FA. Tel: (01344) 711000.

Informix Software UK, Informix House, Littleton Road, Ashford, Middx TW15 1TZ. Tel: (01784) 240444.

Logica, 68 Newman Street, London W1A 4SE. Tel: (0171) 637 9111.

Lotus Development UK, Lotus Park, The Causeway, Staines, Middlesex TW18 3AG. Tel: (01784) 469345.

Microsoft UK, Microsoft Park, Winnersh, Wokingham, Berks RG11 5TP. Tel: (01734) 270000.

Novell UK, Avon House, Sweetwell Road, Bracknell, Berks RG12 1HH. Tel: (01344) 860400.

Novus Systems Technology, Southfield House, Broadford Park, Shalford, Guildford, Surrey GU4 8EN. Tel: (01483) 569933; Fax: (01483) 573082.

Olivetti, Olivetti House, Featherstone Road, Wolverton Mill, Milton Keynes MK12 5RF. Fax: (01908) 203464.

Oracle UK, The Oracle Centre, The Ring, Bracknell, Berks RG12 1BW. Tel: (01344) 660066.

Pegasus Software, Orion House, Orion Way, Kettering, Northants NN15 6PE. Tel: (01536) 495001.

Pyramid Technology Ltd, Pyramid House, Solartron Road, Farnborough, Hampshire GU14 7QL. Tel: (01252) 373035; Fax: (01252) 555333.

Recruitment and Assessment Services (IT recruitment centre for the UK Civil Service), Alencon Link, Basingstoke RG21 1JB. Tel: (01256) 846315.

SAP UK, 7 Queen Square, Bedfont Lakes, Feltham, Middlesex TW14 8HA. Tel: (0181) 818 2940.

Siemens Network Systems Ltd, Technology House, Maylands Avenue, Hemel Hempstead, Herts HP2 7DF. Tel: (01442) 883300.

Sybase Software, Sybase House, Bell Street, Maidenhead, Berks SL6 1XW. Tel: (01628) 27222.

Texas Instruments, Littleton Road, Ashford, Middlesex TW15 1TZ. Tel: (01784) 212222.

Unisys Ltd, Stonebridge Park, London NW10 8LS. Tel: (0181) 965 0511).

Vodafone, Freepost RG2039, Newbury, Berkshire RG13 1BR. Tel: (01635) 503001.

COMPUTER RECRUITMENT AGENCIES

Abraxas Computer Services, 357 Euston Road, London NW1 3AL. Tel: (0171) 388 2061; Fax: (0171) 387 3699.

Alltronics People, Unit 2 Windsor Park, 50 Windsor Avenue, London SW19 2RR. Tel: (0181) 543 9394; Fax: (0181) 543 3646.

Apex Computer Recruitment Ltd, Boundary House, 91 Charterhouse Street, London EC1M 6HR. Tel: (0171) 336 7836; Fax: (0171) 336 7731.

ARC International, 15–16 New Burlington Street, London W1X 1FF. Tel: (0171) 287 2525; Fax: (0171) 287 9688.

Arena Resources, Lonsdale House, 7–9 Lonsdale Gardens, Tunbridge Wells, Kent TN1 1NU. Tel: (01892) 525 232; Fax: (01892) 525 233.

ASC Connections Ltd, 601–602 The Big Peg, 120 Vyse Street, Hockley, Birmingham B18 6NF. Tel: (0121) 624 4343; Fax: (0121) 624 3212.

Austen Consultancy Limited, Austen House, 1 Upper Street, Fleet, Hampshire GU13 9PE. Tel: (01252) 816634; Fax: (01252) 811075.

CBS Appointments, Wooton House, Wooton Gardens, Bournemouth, Dorset BH1 1PW. Tel: (01202) 292155; Fax: (01202) 554299.

Certes Computing Ltd, Arthur House, Roman Way, Coleshill, Warwickshire B46 1HQ. Tel: (01675) 467475; Fax: (01675) 467314.

Classic Recruitment, 4th Floor, 15 Bolton Street, London W1Y 8AR. Tel: (0171) 355 3686; Fax: (0171) 355 4667.

Computer 2000, 11 Harley Street, London W1N 2DA. Tel: (0171) 636 7584; Fax: (0171) 580 3734.

Computer Futures, 18–21 Queen Square, Bristol BS1 4NH, Tel: (0117) 988 0000; Fax: (0117) 9750195.

Computer Futures, 2 Fourbert's Place, Regent Street, London W1V 2AD. Tel: (0171) 446 6644.

Computer Futures, Suite 3, Wilmslow House, Grove Way, Wilmslow, Cheshire SK15 1AQ. Tel: (01625) 526000; Fax: (01625) 549966.

Computer People City, Freepost Victory House, 7 Selsdon Way, City Harbour, London E14 9GL. Tel: (0171) 510 2000; Fax: (0171) 510 2292.

Computer People Ireland, Freepost Carmichael House, 60 Lower Baggot Street, Dublin 2, Ireland. Tel: 353 1 6614998; Fax: 353 1 6762664.

Computer People West End, Freepost VU House, 68–69 St Martins Lane, London WC2 4BR. Tel: (0171) 836 8411; Fax: (0171) 497 2935.

Computer People West, Freepost, BM 4226, Bristol Bridge House, Redcliff Street, Bristol BS1 11YS. Tel: (0117) 927 6236; Fax: (0117) 929 1444.

Computer Team, Charter House, 13/15 Carteret Street, London SW1H 9DJ. Tel: (0171) 799 3081; Fax: (0171) 799 3090.

Compuvac, 66 Great Eastern Street, London EC2A 3PP. Tel: (0171) 613 7000; Fax: (0171) 613 7001.

Cope Management IT Recruitment, City Bridge House, 235–245 Goswell Road, London EC1V 7ID.

Cray Systems, 7 Clairmont Gardens, Glasgow G3 7LW. Tel: (0141) 332 9550; Fax: (0141) 332 6734.

Dart Resourcing Group, 20 Norton Folgate, Bishopsgate, London E1 6DB. Tel: (0171) 377 9922; Fax: (0171) 377 6744.

— 4 Unity Street, Bristol, Avon BS1 5HH. Tel: (0117) 9279933; Fax: (0117) 9279932.

— 61a Queen Street, Edinburgh EH2 4NA. Tel: (0131) 220 2833; Fax: (0161) 220 2922.

— Monaco House, Bristol Street, Birmingham B5 7AS. Tel: (0121) 622 4110; Fax: (0121) 622 2045.

— Sunlight House, Quay Street, Manchester M3 3LD. Tel: (0161) 834 0343; Fax: (0161) 8343974.

— The Grove, Slough, Berkshire SL1 1RH. Tel: (01753) 534610; Fax: (01753) 575577.

Datel Staff Contracting, Old Docks House, 90 Watery Lane, Preston PR2 1AU. Tel: (01772) 760600; Fax: (01772) 769922.

Diagonal Computer Services, Quay West, Trafford Wharf Road, Manchester M17 1HH. Tel: (0161) 877 2777; Fax: (0161) 877 9693.

DPP International, 34 The Quadrant, Richmond, Surrey TW9 1DN. Tel: (0181) 332 2555; Fax: (0181) 940 9864.

Eaglecliff Limited, Hermes House, 80–90 Beckenham Road, Beckenham, Kent BR3 4RH. Tel: (0181) 650 8822; Fax: (0181) 658 6083.

Elan Computing, 3rd Floor, Wade House, The Merrion Centre, Leeds LS2 8LY. Tel: (01132) 455322; Fax: (01132) 446076.

Executive Recruitment Services, Boundary Way, Hemel Hempstead, Herts HP2 7RX. Tel: (01442) 231691; Fax: (01442) 230063.

Fernhart Computer Services, 50 Burnhill Road, Beckenham, Kent BR3 3LA. Tel: (0181) 658 7833; Fax: (0181) 658 1726.

Footprint Computer Recruitment, 42 Alfred Place, Kingsdown, Bristol BS2 8HD. Tel: (0117) 441050; Fax: (0117) 441055.

Formula Systems Limited, 1 Grandier Court, Sandecoates Road, Poole, Dorset BH14 8NX. Tel: (01202) 718817; Fax: (01202) 718828.

Frost Berkeley Associates, Epworth House, 25 City Road, London EC1Y 1AA. Tel: (0171) 374 0374; Fax: (0171) 374 4123.

Gatton Computastaff, Gatton Place, St Matthews Road, Redhill, Surrey RH1 1TA. Tel: (01737) 774100; Fax: (01737) 772949.

Genesis Computer Resources, 15 Copthorne Road, Felbridge, East Grinstead RH19 2NR. Tel: (01342) 311181; Fax: (01342) 311184.

Harvey Nash PLC, Dragon Court, 27–29 Macklin Street, London WC2B 5LX. Tel: (0171) 333 0033; Fax: (0171) 333 0032.

Hayden Pearse Group Ltd, 61 Cheapside, London EC2V 6BU. Tel: (0171) 236 0151; Fax: (0171) 236 2888.

Hexagon Computer Services, Hexagon House, 145 Wardour Street, London W1V 3TB. Tel: (0171) 439 3671; Fax: (0171) 734 0503.

Hunterskil Ltd, St James House, Vicar Lane, Sheffield S1 2EX. Tel: (0345) 252020; Fax: (0114) 275 3933.

Huxley Associates, 2 Conduit Street, London W1R 9TG. Tel: (0171) 409 2300; Fax: (0171) 409 1499.

IBS Consulting Services, 2 Bath Street, London EC1V 9DX. Tel: (0171) 454 9822; Fax: (0171) 454 9827.

James Duncan Associates, Seabridge House, 8 St Johns Road, Tunbridge Wells, Kent TN4 9NP. Tel: (01892) 544757; Fax: (01892) 547273.

JCC Contracts, 106 London Road, St Albans, Herts AL1 1NX. Tel: (01727) 836361; Fax: (01727) 860033.

Kenda Systems Limited, Adamson House, Market Place, Manchester M3 1RE. Tel: (0161) 833 9341; Fax: (0161) 833 0171.

Kudos, 10 Westminster Court, Hipley Street, Woking, Surrey GU22 9LQ. Tel: (01483) 747227; Fax: (01483) 747337.

Mapp Computer Consultants Ltd, Wing House, Britannia Street, Aylesbury, Buckinghamshire HP20 1QS. Tel: (01296) 28661; Fax: (01296) 393923.

Matchmaker Personnel Limited, 1590 Parkway, Solent Business

Park, Whiteley, Fareham PO15 7AG. Tel: (01489) 579079; Fax: (01489) 579279.

Modus International, The Tythe Barn, High Street, Edlesborough, Dunstable, Bedfordshire LU6 2HS. Tel: (01525) 222222; Fax: (01525) 222466.

Montreal Associates, City Gate House, 399–425 Eastern Avenue, Gants Hill, Ilford, Essex IG2 6LR. Tel: (0181) 5182211; Fax: (0181) 5183898.

MVM Recruitment Ltd, MVM HOUSE, 2 Oakfield Road, Clifton, Bristol BS8 2AL. Tel: (0117) 970 6898; Fax: (0117) 970 6891.

Myriad IT and Technical Resourcing, 25 South Street, Reading, Berks RG1 4QU. Tel: (01734) 591151; Fax: (01734) 503954.

— 3 Haig Court, Haig Road, Knutsford, Cheshire WA16 8XZ. Tel: (01565) 750450; Fax: (01565) 750452.

— 30 Fleet Street, London EC4Y 1AA. Tel: (0171) 583 2110; Fax: (0171) 353 5868.

— 40 Old Market Street, Bristol BS2 0EZ. Tel: (0117) 9291040; Fax: (0117) 925 0297.

— The Courtyard, Alban Park, Harfield Road, St Albans AL4 0LA. Tel: (01727) 845818; Fax: (01727) 845922.

Nesco, 98 Weaver Street, Winsford, Cheshire CW7 4AE. Tel: (01606) 550163; Fax: (01606) 593739.

Nescomms Ltd, St James Business Centre, Linwood Road, Paisley, Glasgow PA3 3AT. Tel: (0141) 848 0440; Fax: (0141) 848 7745.

Oldham and Tomkins Ltd, 3 High Street, Windsor, Berks SL4 1LD. Tel: (01753) 850007; Fax: (01753) 857449.

Oric Computer Personnel, 188 Shoreditch High Street, London E1 6HU. Tel: (0171) 729 7329; Fax: (0171) 739 5049.

Outsource UK, Freepost SN1 085, Swindon SN2 2UR. Tel: (01793) 430021; Fax: (01793) 432337.

Paragon IT Human Resources, The Business Design Centre, 52 Upper Street, London N1 0QH. Tel: (0171) 288 6247; Fax: (0171) 288 6248.

PC People, 1 St Colme Street, Edinburgh EH3 6AA. Tel: (0131) 220 8231; Fax: (0131) 220 3448.

People In Computers, 35 Alfred Place, London WC1E 7DP. Tel: (0171) 636 2211; Fax: (0171) 636 2299.

Perpetual Resources Ltd, Barnwell House, Barnwell Drive, Cambridge CB5 8UU. Tel: (01223) 240799; Fax: (01223) 244701.

Profile Computer Recruitment, 18 Orchard Croft, Barnt Green, Birmingham B45 8NH. Tel: (0121) 445 3727.

Progressive Computer Recruitment, Europa House, 266–276 Upper Richmond Road, London SW15 6TQ. Tel: (0181) 785 3333; Fax: (0181) 780 0207.

PSP Ltd, 9th Floor, Swan Office Centre, Coventry Road, Yardley, Birmingham B25 8AD. Tel: (0121) 706 7672; Fax: (0121) 708 2727.

Real Time Consultants Plc. 118–120 Warwick Street, Royal Leamington Spa, Warwickshire CV32 4QY. Tel: (01926) 313133; Fax: (01926) 422165.

Reed Direct Access, Freepost SL757, Talworth Tower, Talworth, Surrey KT6 7BR. Tel: 0500 353637.

Resources International PLC, 31 Bedford Square, London WC1B 3EG. Tel: (0171) 314 4200; Fax: (0171) 323 3094.

RMW 27 Bridge Road, Hampton Court, Surrey KT8 9EU. Tel: (0181) 941 2101; Fax: (0181) 941 5242.

Rullion Computer Personnel Ltd, Trafalgar House, 110 Manchester Road, Altrincham, Cheshire WA14 1NU. Tel: (0161) 941 5335; Fax: (0161) 929 9791.

S-Com, Buckingham House, Buckingham Street, Aylesbury HP20 2LA. Tel: (01296) 311411; Fax: (01296) 436895.

Sanderson Contract Recruitment, Somerset House, 18 Canynge Road, Clifton, Bristol BS8 3LJ. Tel: (0117) 973 3339; Fax: (0117) 9733 883.

Search Recruitment and Selection, 1A Hill Street, Edinburgh EH2 3JP. Tel: (0131) 226 4444; Fax: (0131) 226 4443.

Software 92 PLC, 7 Trinity Place, Midland Drive, Sutton Coldfield, Birmingham B72 1TX. Tel: (0121) 354 9911; Fax: (0121) 543 1565.

The Agency Partnership, 6 Leck House, Lake Street, Leighton Buzzard, Beds LU7 8TQ. Tel: (01525) 853550; Fax: (01525) 851768.

The Eurolink Group PLC, 6 Hope Street, Edinburgh EH2 4DB. Tel: (0131) 220 0420; Fax: (0131) 220 1973.

The Macleod Group, 11–15 High Street, Marlow, Bucks SL7 1AU. Tel: (01628) 890313; Fax: (01628) 890198.

The Span Consultancy, 44 Great Windmill Street, London W1V 7PA. Tel: (0171) 734 7394; Fax: (0171) 734 8756.

TLP PLC, Robert Denholm House, Betchingly Road, Nutfield, Surrey RH1 4HW. Tel: (01737) 824000; Fax: (01737) 824001

Trinity Expert Systems Ltd, 32 Richmond Road, Olton, Solihull B92 7RP. Tel: (01203) 424508; Fax: (01203) 425187.

Valentine Scott, PO BOX 8155, London W2 2GW. Tel: (0171) 486 0486; Fax: (0171) 486 1608.

Vantage Recruitment, Acorn House, Midsummer Boulevard, Milton Keynes MK9 3HP. Tel: (01908) 691400; Fax: (01908) 691155.

VNG Nationwide, 13–14 Park Place, Leeds LS1 2SJ. Tel: (0113) 245 1442; Fax: (0113) 243 4528.

COMPUTER RECRUITMENT AGENCIES FOR OVERSEAS JOBS

(*Australia*) Comtex, 40–41 Old Bond Street, London W1X 3AF. Tel: (0171) 629 6155; Fax: (0171) 629 6047.

(*Australia, NZ, USA, Europe*) CCA, 80 Bedford Court Mansions, Bedford Avenue, London WC1B 3AE. Tel: (0171) 436 1565; Fax: (0171) 323 0846.

(*Europe/Hong Kong*) Clivedon Technical Recruitment, 92 Broadway, Bracknell, Berks RG12 1AR. Tel: (01344) 489489; Fax: (01344) 489505.

(*Europe/International*) Computer People West End, Freepost VU House, 68–69 St Martins Lane, London WC2 4BR. Tel: (0171) 836 8411; Fax: (0171) 497 2935.

(*Europe/International*) Gatton Computastaff, Gatton Place, St Matthews Road, Redhill, Surrey RH1 1TA. Tel: (01737) 774100; Fax: (01737) 772949.

(*Europe/USA*) Dataforce International Ltd, 22 Four Oaks Road, Sutton Coldfield, West Midlands B74 2TH. Tel: (0121) 308 2521.

(*Europe/USA*) SRA (Europe) BV, 500 Chesham House, 150 Regent Street, London W1R 5FA. Tel: (0171) 439 6288; Fax: (0171) 995 7742.

(*Europe/USA*) SBS, 22 Bloomsbury Square, London WC1A 2NS. Tel: (0171) 580 2355; Fax: (0171) 636 9170.

(*Europe/USA*) Hestair Computer Group plc, Premier House, 1 Canning Road, Harrow, Middlesex HA3 7TS. Tel: (0181) 863 0049; Fax: (0181) 861 3139.

(*Europe, Far East, Australia*) EPL, 51 Clarence Road, Windsor, Berks SL4 3AX. Tel: (01753) 8330017; Fax: (01753) 864358.

(*Europe, mainly Holland*) Tangent International, Shelduck House,

10 Woodbrook Crescent, Billericay, Essex CM12 0EQ. Tel: (01277) 630055; Fax: (01277) 633133.

(*Europe, USA, Middle East*) James Baker Associates, Park House, Wick Road, Egham, Surrey TW20 0HW. Tel: (01784) 473347; Fax: (01784) 438181.

(*Europe, USA*) BCL International, Clerks Court, 18–20 Farringdon Lane, London EC1R 3AU. Tel: (0171) 251 1125; Fax: (0171) 251 4902.

(*Europe*) Abbeywood International, Thornton House, Thornton Road, Wimbledon, London SW19 4NG. Tel: (0181) 944 6688; Fax: (0181) 944 6841.

(*Europe*) Arena Resources, The Coach House, London Road, Hurst Green, East Sussex TN19 7QP. Tel: (01580) 860860; Fax: (01580) 860861.

(*Europe*) CSS Hamilton House, Marlowes, Hemel Hempstead, Herts HP1 1BR. Tel: (01442) 240761; Fax: (01442) 259997.

(*Europe*) Dart Resourcing Group, Rue Capitaine, Crespel 47, Boite 44 1050, Belgium. Tel: + +322 548 9400; Fax: + +322 548 9419.

(*Europe*) Elan Computing Ltd, 93 Newman Street, London W1P 4DS. Tel: (0171) 830 1300; Fax: (0171) 830 1333.

(*Europe*) EuroSkill Resource Ltd, Langsmeade House, Milton Common, Oxon OX9 2JY. Tel: (01844) 279033; Fax: (01844) 279256.

(*Europe*) IC Software, Hamilton House, The Marlowes, Hemel Hempstead, Herts HP1 1BB. Tel: (01442) 234 243; Fax: (01442) 234 207.

(*Europe*) MBA, 1 Willow Street, London EC2A 4BH. Tel: (0171) 739 2022; Fax: (0171) 739 2129.

(*Europe*) TLP Marktonderoek, Nederland BY, Singel 120, 1015 AE Amsterdam, Netherlands. Tel: 0031 20 4202666; Fax: 0031 20 6237902.

(*Mainly USA*) Abraxas Computer Services, 357 Euston Road, London NW1 3AL. Tel: (0171) 388 2061; Fax: (0171) 387 3699.

(*Mediterranean Europe*) Appointments International, 4 Glencairn, 70 Ridgeway, London SW19 4RA. Fax only: (0181) 946 5722.

(*New Zealand, Europe*) A & P Computer Services, 14 Leicester Road, New Barnet, Herts EN5 5DA. Tel: (0181) 449 9496; Fax: (0181) 449 6357.

(*Saudi Arabia*) Arabian Careers, 115 Shaftsbury Avenue, London WC2H 8AD. Tel: (0171) 379 7877; Fax: (0171) 379 0855.

(*USA, Canada, Australia*) Eurolink Group PLC, 56 Old Steins, Brighton BN1 1NH. Tel: (01273) 202316; Fax: (01273) 723078.

(*USA, Europe*) Worldsearch Ltd, 11th Floor, Regent House, Heaton Lane, Stockport SK4 1BS. Tel: (0161) 480 9566; Fax: (0161) 476 1758.

(*USA, Mexico, Puerto Rico*) Prime Selection, 136 Kentish Town Road, London NW1 9QB. Tel: (0171) 419 2525; Fax: (0171) 482 4239.

(*USA*) Computech International Resources, 34 Francis Grove, Wimbledon, London SW19 4DY. Tel: (0181) 288 4880; Fax: (0181) 288 4882.

(*USA*) Datatronics USA, Premier House, 11 Marlborough Place, Brighton BN1 1UB. Tel: (01273) 624943; Fax: (01273) 698977.

(*USA*) DJ Recruitment, 74 Tongdean Lane, Brighton BN1 5JE. Tel: (01273) 506457; Fax: (01273) 507141.

(*USA*) The Kingfisher Consultancy, PO BOX 2556, Bridge House, 22 Bromsgrove Road, Redditch, Worcs B97 4AA. Tel: (0527) 595700; Fax: (0527) 595720.

(*Worldwide*) Computer People International, Piccadilly House, 33 Regent Street, London W1Y 4NB. Tel: (0171) 287 0050; Fax: (0171) 287 0785.

(*Worldwide*) LA International, Ridge House, Ridge House Drive, Festival Park, Stoke on Trent ST1 5SJ. Tel: (01782) 279099; Fax: (01782) 273919.

FINDING WORK ABROAD AND HELP FOR NON UK NATIONALS LOOKING FOR WORK IN THE UK

The Employment Service, Overseas Placing Unit, 4th Floor, Steel City House, c/o Moorfoot, Sheffield S1 4PQ. Tel: (01742) 596051/2.

The Department of Employment, Overseas Labour Section, Caxton House, Tothill Street, London SW1H 9NA. Tel: (0171) 273 5336.

The Home Office, Immigration and Nationality Department, Lunar House, Wellesley Road, Croydon CR9 2BY. Tel: (0181) 686 0688.

SOME COMMERCIAL COMPANIES OFFERING COMPUTER TRAINING AND EDUCATION COURSES

Hoskyns Group, Glen House, Stag Place, London SW1E 5AG. Tel: (0171) 830 6830—write or phone for a free training directory.

QA Training, Cecily Hill Castle, Cirencester, Gloucestershire GL7 2EF. Tel: (01285) 650537—write or phone for free training directory.

Computer Associates, 183/187 Bath Road, Slough, Berkshire SL1 4AA. Tel: (01753) 679679.

Oracle Training Services—over 100 course titles in nine regional centres across the UK. Tel: (0345) 777711.

IR Services, 88 Ashburton Road, Hugglescote, Coalville, Leicester LE67 2HB. Tel: (01530) 810075.

See also the list of universities given elsewhere in this section. In addition to degree level and full time vocational courses, many also offer part time, less expensive and more practical 'hands on' computer related training courses.

Index

HOW TO USE THE INTERNET
A practical introduction for every computer user

Granam Jones

The fast-growing Internet is set to revolutionise personal and business communications across the globe, as well as entertainment, information and education. Unlike other books on 'The Net', here is a down to earth practical guide that will help you get the most out of this communication revolution. Gone are the heavy technical introductions, the in-depth computer instructions. Instead, here are simple straightforward steps that anyone can use to get onto the Net and start exploring the new information super highway. Soon, nearly everyone in the developed world will have access to the Internet. This book shows you how and where to begin. Graham Jones is a leading business consultant and author. He is Managing Director of a specialist business that utilises the Internet for up-to-date information.

126pp illus. 1 85703 197 0.

HOW TO WRITE & SELL COMPUTER SOFTWARE
A practical guide to creating and marketing software ideas

Stephen Harding

Premium quality software always sells. Crucial to today's business, and continually sought by home users, there is always plenty of room in the market for a well designed and easy to use new software package. This book is for people who want to write and sell their own software, either to make a living or just a useful part-time income. From business software to computer games, this book explains how to identify and research the market, how to plan and prepare a quality software product for launch, how to package, advertise and distribute your product, how to attract and stimulate customer interest and, most important of all, how to sell it, build a customer base and operate a successful and professional software business. Steve Harding is the director of a successful software company. He has fifteen years' professional experience writing and selling computer software.

160pp illus. 1 85703 214 4.

HOW TO PREPARE A BUSINESS PLAN
Laying the right foundations for business success

Matthew Record

A business plan is the most important commercial document you will ever have to produce, whether you are just starting out in business, or are already trading. A well thought out and carefully structured plan will be crucial to the survival and longterm success of the enterprise. It will provide a detailed map of exactly where it is going, and help you forestall any problems long before they arise. A third of all new businesses fail in their first year, and of the rest a staggering 95 per cent will not make it beyond 5 years. Poor planning has been identified as the major cause of business failure. With the odds so stacked against success, make sure YOUR business gets off to the right start. Matthew Record is a business consultant specialising in the preparation of business plans for a variety of commercial clients. His company, Phoenix Business Plans, is based in Dorset.

158pp illus. 1 85703 178 4.

STARTING TO MANAGE
How to prepare yourself for a more responsible role at work

Julie-Ann Amos

Management is not in itself difficult. The problem is, it isn't always easy, either. This practical introduction gives a broad overview of management, to dispel much of the mystery which surrounds it. It is intended for all new managers, supervisors, students and anyone who hopes to enter management. It explains the various basic theories surrounding management, and puts these into a practical everyday context. The reader will learn how to manage workloads, decisions, stock, equipment, money, legislation, customers, staff, and much more besides. The book will make an ideal launch pad for everyone wanting to start taking responsibility and influence events in their own organisation. Julie-Ann Amos is a graduate of the Universities of East Anglia and Portsmouth, and Member of the Institute of Personnel and Development. She is a Senior Personnel Officer and Trainer with a large local authority, and has post-graduate qualifications in both Personnel and Administrative Management.

160pp illus. 1 85703 319 1.

HOW TO MANAGE COMPUTERS AT WORK
A step-by-step guide for beginners

Graham Jones

Here is a practical step-by-step guide which puts the business needs of the user first. It discusses why a computer may be needed, how to choose the right one and instal it properly; how to process letters and documents, manage accounts, and handle customer and other records and mailing lists. It also explains how to use computers for business presentations, and desktop publishing. If you feel you should be using a computer at work, but are not sure how to start, then this is definitely the book for you . . . and you won't need an electronics degree to start! 'Bags of information in a lingo we call all understand. I strongly recommend the book.' *Progress/NEBS Management Association.* Graham Jones has long experience of handling personal computers for small business management. The Managing Director of a desktop publishing company, he is also author of *How to Start a Business from Home* and *How to Publish a Newsletter* in this Series.

160pp 1 85703 078 8.

HOW TO START YOUR OWN BUSINESS
Planning and creating a successful enterprise

Jim Green

This dynamic guide fully explores the vital steps to creating a business, interlaced with the author's recent experience in overcoming every hurdle encountered along the way in setting up his own business without capital or discretionary resources. It will show you how to galvanise into initial action, how to source proven ideas, how to write a winning plan, how to approach potential funders, how to present a case for public sector assistance, how to market your business and how to develop the selling habit. No matter what your age or personal circumstances, you *can* strike out on your own, create an enterprise and change your life for the better. Jim Green is chairman and managing director of Focus Publishing International Ltd and for many years specialised in founding, buying and selling advertising agencies.

159pp illus. 1 85703 122 9.

MANAGING MEETINGS
How to prepare, how to take part and how to follow up

Ann Dobson

Meetings can be interesting, productive and even fun! That is the message this new 'How To' book seeks to convey. Meetings form a large part of our lives today, particularly in the business world, yet many of us feel ill equipped to handle them with ease. The book is divided into two parts: the first covers the key skills of communicating effectively, motivating and persuading, problem solving, decision making, body language, and dealing with troublemakers. Part 2 deals with the practical steps of holding a meeting and following up. Case studies, self-assessment material and checklists complete the simple, yet effective approach. Ann Dobson is Principal of a Secretarial Training School, and has been involved with meetings of varying types for many years. She is also the author of *How to Communicate at Work, How to Write Business Letters, How to Return to Work* and *How to Manage an Office* in this series.

128pp illus. 1 85703 222 5.

HOW TO MANAGE PEOPLE AT WORK
A practical guide to effective leadership

John Humphries

'These days, if a textbook on people management is to succeed, it must be highly informative, reliable, comprehensive—and eminently user-friendly. Without doubt, *How to Manage People at Work* is one such book. Written in an attractive style that should appeal to any first-line manager who has neither the time nor the energy to cope with heavy reading, John Humphries has tackled his extremely wide subject ably and well. Rightly or wrongly, it has always been my experience that one has only to read the first couple of pages of any textbook on people management to discover whether or not the author enjoys an empathy with the people at the sharp end—and here is one author who, for my money, has passed the test with flying colours.' *Progress/NEBS Management Association.*

160pp illus. 1 85703 068 0. 2nd edition.

MANAGING YOURSELF
How to achieve your personal goals in life and at work

Julie-Ann Amos

Managing yourself is often more difficult than it seems. So many other people, events and things seem to take control of, exert influence over, or just interfere with our lives and how we want to behave. This simple book goes beyond assertiveness and behaviour, and examines how to deal *inside* ourselves with the daily conflicts of everyday life. The reader will learn how to handle criticism, thoughts and emotions, aggression, passivity, change, conflict, and stress, through developing assertive communications and listening skills, body language and confidence. Julie-Ann Amos is a Member of the Institute of Personnel and Development. She is a Senior Personnel Officer and Trainer with a large local authority, and has taught Assertiveness and Personal Effectiveness programmes for many years. She has post-graduate qualifications in both Personnel and Administrative Management.

160pp illus. 1 85703 324 8.

HOW TO COUNSEL PEOPLE AT WORK
A practical approach to staff care

John Humphries

The value of counselling has become much better recognised in recent times, as a tool for addressing a whole variety of human situations. This new book has been specially written for everyone wanting to know how to make use of counselling techniques in the workplace. It discusses what is counselling, the role of the counsellor, communication skills, body language/verbal behaviour, styles of counselling, managing counselling interviews, and the uses of counselling. The book is complete with helpful checklists, case studies, self-assessment material and points for discussion, key addresses, glossary and index.

104pp illus. 1 85703 093 1.

HOW TO KEEP BUSINESS ACCOUNTS
A handbook for business owners, managers and students

Peter Taylor

The third fully revised edition of an easy-to-understand handbook for all business owners and managers. 'Will help you sort out the best way to carry out double entry book-keeping, as well as providing a clear step-by-step guide to accounting procedures.' *Mind Your Own Business.* 'Progresses through the steps to be taken to maintain an effective double entry book-keeping system with the minimum of bother.' *The Accounting Technician.* 'Compulsory reading.' *Manager, National Westminster Bank (Midlands).* Peter Taylor is a Fellow of the Institute of Chartered Accountants. He has many years' practical experience of advising small businesses.

176pp illus. 1 85703 111 3. 3rd edition.

HOW TO EMPLOY & MANAGE STAFF
A practical handbook for managers and supervisors

Wendy Wyatt

Now in a revised second edition, this easy to use handbook is intended for all young managers, supervisors and students whose work will involve them in recruiting and managing staff. Ideal for quick reference, it provides a ready-made framework of modern employment practice from recruitment onwards. It provides a clear account of how to apply the health & safety at work regulations, how to handle record-keeping, staff development, grievance and disciplinary procedures, maternity and sick leave and similar matters for the benefit of the organisation and its employees. The book includes a useful summary of current employment legislation and is complete with a range of model forms, letters, notices and similar documents. Wendy Wyatt MIPD is a Personnel Management and Employment Consultant; her other books include *Recruiting Success* and *Jobhunt.*

176pp illus. 1 85703 167 9. 2nd edition.